WHEN THE HEART HOLDS ITS BREATH

SALWA ASIF

Printed in the USA, 2025

Library of Congress Cataloging-in-Publication Data
Salwa Asif
     When The Heart Holds Its Breath by Salwa Asif.
     ISBN: 979-8-89972-014-7

For information or permissions, contact:
[salwaaasif@gmail.com]

Dedications

To the ones who stayed soft through the breaking,
who kept breathing even when it hurt…

this is for you…

and for the version of me
who needed this book to exist.

And above all, this is for Allah,
for the nur that found me in the dark,
and never let me go.

Acknowledgements

This book waited inside me for years
– through silence, ache, healing, and returning.

I wrote it in pieces, in prayers, in pauses.
I wrote it when I didn't know if I'd ever share it,
and again when I realized I had to.

To *my parents* – thank you for being my roots, my
compass, and the quiet strength behind everything
I've ever dared to do.
This book is yours too.

To *my best friend, Abdallah* – your presence, loyalty,
and belief in me came like calm in the middle of
noise.
Thank you for always seeing me.

To *my sister* – I carry you in every word.
I wish you could read this, but maybe you already
have.
This is for the both of us.

To the ones who listened when my voice trembled.
To those who saw me in stillness and stayed
– you helped me remember who I was when I forgot.

Contents

A Little Light

You are the smile to my lips,
You are the melody to my heart.

The fire ignites the ego, looking towards the shine-
Without a simple glance behind.
Feet readily walk on the blanket of blazing fire.

The storm that meant to crush like a damaged can-
Rather ignites the dead holes into cracking fireworks.

Rainstorms creating streams of darkness-
Dissolve in the prevailing dawn of fierce firestorms.

Hardships come with unexpected luck and bucket of
cheers,
Comprehend the faith and tear out like shooting stars,
Enlighten hope rather than destroying the angels!

The magical melody in every nook and corner made
the devils meet,
Soon stroked in the stone heart, numbness infinite!

A Quiet Departure

How sad was the departure,
Like a flower without its fragrance,
Like sleep without relief,
Like a night without twinkling stars.

Reflecting on my life,
Tears trickle down my cheeks.
My lips force a smile, but my heart denies the need,
And the little sadness seems sweet in this solemn
ambiance.

When the memories claw back,
The heart of me weeps—
For those warm evenings long past,
For those joyous treks,
For a lullaby that once calmed the storm inside.

How I yearn for what was,
Yet I wander on,
Sitting alone in the stillness,
Where shadows speak of things left behind.

The Unspoken Wish

Woken late,
Chasing a dream not yet touched,
She works quietly,
Her talent weaving through the hours.

Her eyes, tired but awake,
Ached bones beneath the weight of desire,
Yet her pen moves steadily,
As though the world might listen.

What joy could her life hold,
She wonders as her thoughts unfold,
A gentle excitement stirs within,
Eyes reflecting a soft, unspoken wish.

Closing her notebook,
She murmurs a prayer,
Hands cupped, feeling the peace,
Sending her hopes on a quiet journey,
Trusting they'll find their place.

And there, she rests,
A calm smile brushing her lips,
As though a quiet hope whispers within her,
That her efforts will not be in vain.

A Part of Me

Reflecting on my life
Tears trickle down my cheeks.
My lips force a smile, but my heart denies the need.
In the memory of a love so tender,
A connection I thought would never fade.

How elegant you were,
More radiant than the rest,
A presence that filled every space,
Moving through life with an energy that was all your
own.
How I miss the warmth you brought,
I wish you had never left.

You were as wise as an owl,
Learning the language of my heart in no time,
Coming to me like an old friend whenever I called,
Addicted to the simple joys, living fully in every
moment.
You were deep, spiritual, intelligent, and full of love,
But a spark of mischief, always stirring the calm.

How I miss the little things—
Your quiet moments, your head resting in peace,
The way you climbed through life with such ease,
Your bemused smile, your joyful face when you saw
me,
So captivated by the rhythms of human company,
You stirred everything, making the world feel alive.

Perhaps it was easier to lock you away,
To silence the chaos you sometimes brought,
But then, one day, you simply vanished,
Leaving behind a space that nothing could fill.
I searched for you, but no trace was found,
Yet I still feel your presence in the places you once
graced.

Maybe you are out there, living your own story,
A quiet spirit, free and unbound,
A part of me, always remembered, forever loved.

Âme Damnée

Flying high in the sky,
Like a black kite,
Cawing endlessly,
Infuriating all who hear.

How loathsome is that bird,
Quivering with pride,
Convinced it is the best,
Yet deemed nothing but ugly.

Curses cast upon it,
Like scurrying cockroaches,
Unwanted, despised,
A target for mockery.

But place yourself in its wings—
How would you feel?
The world should pause,
And understand this truth:
Not all that glitters is gold.

Another Chance

Loyalty fills the hearts,
The path of love unfolds before us.
You called it honestly,
I felt it like a mallet striking a chisel in my heart—
A child of illusion, a parent of disillusion.

You showed every season,
While I knew only spring.
Like measles, I bore it alone—
The warfare of flames and burning coal.
You crushed my heart like a giant pigeon,
Wings flapping without care.

Sometimes, the rain ignited hope,
Other times, we tasted madness.
Let's lose ourselves where the winds of love blow,
Become strangers and meet again.
Let's reverse time, avoid the termites,
And teach each other how to live again.
Nothing would ever break the spark.

Be Yourself

Be yourself, no matter what,
People are never quite content.
No matter how much love is sought,
Jealousy will still be present—
That's the human nature, bent.

Never underestimate your worth,
For others' words may cloud your view.
They criticize to prove their mirth,
And degrade to lift themselves anew.
Don't dumb yourself to fit their shoe.

If you want to do what's right,
Though others frown or shake their head,
Do it because it feels so bright—
It's your life, and you're ahead.
Let your dreams soar, not misled.

The paintbrush is yours to hold,
So paint your life with colors bold.
Rise like a star above the rest,
Shine through, put your heart to the test.
Face the world, face your quest,
Embrace the dark and be your best.

Work for awe, and chase the flame,
The critics' words will fall in shame.
For those who scorn one day will see,
The praises will return to thee.
So go on—don't stop the fight,
The fireball is yours; ignite the night.

Beautiful Aroma

Knowledge shapes the soul,
Like a chisel carving stone,
Thoughts unfold the gates of bluestone,
But words, truly, are miracles of their own.

Life once so unorganized,
Wandering hopeless, like a cloud of night,
Just like those ignorant, defiant minds,
Proud of their so-called knowledge, blind to the light.

The beautiful aroma changed it all,
As spring transforms the fall,
Life became organized and bright,
Like those brilliant, glowing minds in flight.

How light she felt,
When those hideous words were penned,
For she had found a remedy to her loneliness,
A key to spread her wings and happiness without
end.

And then, she smirked sweetly in freedom's embrace,
Like—a clever thief planning its next chase.

Beautiful Scars

Away from it all,
Hidden from the world,
Drifting deep within her thoughts,
Trying to escape her past.

The girl who has already had enough,
With no more strength to love again,
No longer hope to be loved again,
She longs to be invisible, just for a while.

She can't trust anyone with that place,
Where once she blindly allowed him in,
Where once she loved him unconditionally,
Where once she dreamed of their future.

And now, she is afraid—
Afraid of everyone,
Needing to keep her distance
From all those selfish motives.
She is afraid!

Afraid of getting hurt,
Afraid of being played again,
Afraid of being used once more,
Afraid of reminiscing her beautiful scars.

Black Rose

I see thorns; I see roses,
Intentionally continue my way on roses,
I let myself drown in the pool of the devil,
Where sinners unintentionally feed the evil,
Un-knowingly I prepare the larking soul for a painful
death,
Consuming unwanted sins with every breath,
How often do we forget the wages of sin?
Enjoying the lust degrading the ego in sinbin,
My conscience knowingly ignores the perception,
Diving ecstatically in the deepest of misconceptions,
Denying the Divine rules, I feel stabbed; I feel feeble,
Carried away by the ardor, I feel jabbed, yet able,
Be a good Samaritan and toil for your goals,
Being a righteous you, you will face thorns and
burning coals,
The good doer has the heaven in eternity,
Envied by devils disguised as angels in this disastrous
pity,
For once, you walk the path of thorns,
Limitless idyllic soothe awaits in the beyond.

Break of Dawn

How upsetting was the severance?
Thy Lord gave to híe,
When Jochebed departed Moses in the Iteru,
My heart was living from hand to mouth,
The shadow faded in thin air towards the south,
I could find no cure in the ambiance so pure,
Soul deemed dead like a child wrongfully led,
Towards love, greed was paid no heed,
Words quickly revealed and spread,
Soon lost mysteriously like a magic spell unread,
In those eyes, she could see demons; she could see
angels,
Overwhelmed by harsh perplexity,
Spontaneous recidivism abruptly conquered by
agonism,
I stubbornly accept that life is a journey,
Nostalgia breaking me down,
Insidious as the break of dawn,
Every journey where I have bled,
Karma, there will be furious red,
To my Lord, I pour my trust,
Once lost in the endless mist.

Flock of Birds

All alone in the world, astonished by the swarm of
souls,
Accompanied by jolts, a sensation of uneasiness in my
control,

Nervousness at its peak; cornered by silent observers,
I found a quiet space where, for spare moments, I
contemplated,

Gone mad by the myriad of desires, the light left me
hazy,
Watching the laughter of others, I yearned for one,

Until my gaze caught you amidst the flickering
sparks, like a beacon,
A companion I always longed for, a bond few are
granted,
Your presence shattered my solitude,

Your support nourished the mystery I was becoming,
How wondrously the connection grew, obeying its
own unseen laws,
You and I, like brilliant fireballs in the endless sea.

I Wonder Why

I wonder why no one can hear
That heartbeat pounding in fragile ears,
I wonder why no one can see
That longing for love, that thirst for care.

I wonder why no one notices
The blood-red sclera, stained not just with pain,
But with the weight, the tension,
Carried by trembling nerves, worn and strained.

I wonder why no one sees
The solitary footprints in the shifting sands,
Screaming silently for aid,
Only to be swallowed by the tide at dusk.

I wonder why no one understands
The voice caught in the wind's whisper,
Trying to stand tall in a sea of uncertainty,
Yet always returning to the shore of mockery.

I wonder why no one grieves
For the restless mind, writhing in the dark,
The years of innocence shattered,
Wandering like a phantom who's lost its spark.

I wonder why no one's astonished
By the silence of lips once full of words,
Now sealed forever, since the storm passed —
The ones who were left with nothing but the wind.

I wonder why no one supports
That tiny, fragile form speaking to the stars,
Finding solace in their distant glow,
Believing them to be the only family left.

I wonder why no hearts break
For that lost soul, adrift in the world,
Wandering like a fading star,
Is it because he's poor,
Or has the world grown to belong only to the rich
now?

Endless Mist

Struggling in the scorching desert heat,
I became a lifeless tree.
My mind was aware of galaxies,
But pockets filled with light air.

The lioness was numb,
Totes lost among the explosion of bombs.
The playful deer was now sitting cowardly,
Frightened from its shadow in this co-operative
comedy.

The dust of the heat hid the sun,
My neck burnt even though the hair was in a spiral
bun.
Dropped corns cooked fiercely in the hot pressure
cooker,
I was hooked in the unpleasant hot breeze.

That brushed through me as a howler.
I flew in a gale to a world very beyond,
Where ominous clouds and pale skies hugged in a
fraction of a second.

A beam of light shone far away,
Guiding the guild through the darkest way,
There, the enemies met, and the lovers reminisced,
Those days of glory that were now missed.

Garments of garnet were garnered to be garbed,
Soon hidden in the abyss, not kept being robbed!

Water raged like a fire.
The air carried the bubbles- entirely burnt.
Heat equivalent to fifty thousand years; not on rent.

How often do I crave for the bliss of solitude?
That is lost amidst the pool of pride.
My soul dies for its destination,
Struggling to determine its achievements.

Merely out of hand,
The heart gasps for breath,
Unfortunately dies in the unknown nation of
thoughts.

Constant Illusion

Feeling absolutely nothing,
I've lost myself in search of me,
Watching myself slip from my own grasp,
The darkness has swallowed me whole.
I am lost—
Totes lost.
I am in desperate need of light.

I want to scream, to break, to let it all out,
I want the light to fill me, cleanse me,
Shield me, guide me,
I want to battle the shadows that haunt me each
night.
I want to remember them, their whispers sharp and
clear,
I want to see them fade into nothingness.

I want to be a bird among the prisoners,
Free, soaring high above the rest.
Something disturbs me,
Something indescribable,
This feeling—so foolish, so ugly, so terrifying.

I want to fly away,
Fly away,
Fly away.

You Never Forget

You will never forget. Memories are permanent.
Good memories bring a smile,
Bad ones come with heartaches.
You never truly forget a memory—
You simply learn how to live with them.

Good memories strengthen the conscience,
Bad memories feed the ego.
Both, taken positively, can shape the best within us.
Both, taken with grace, can be miraculous.

Never let bad memories degrade you.
Face them—dive into the deepest oceans,
And soar to the highest skies.
Let your soul be an open book,
And your heart, the key to perception.

Let your eyes be windows to your disguised
happiness.
Hold the sleeve, not the hand.

Sometimes, you have no control over the bad
memories.
Cry your heart out—
For in that, you learn how to deal with them.
Don't let them alter the path to your success.

Internal Compass

Follow your inner voice,
Follow your internal compass,
Learn to differentiate between the real cries and the
false alarms,
The realistic mind is sometimes the greatest critic of
the impulsive heart,
To a vale of gurgling brooks where flowers-laden
boughs hang low,
It is a monster lurking in the already tired heart,
Step out of your meandering moods,
Learn to live outside the bubble of your frequent
fears,
Challenge the aching apprehensions,
Fascinate the brewing boredom,
Creativity is a strong motivator,
A whirlpool of mundane repetitiveness,
Prevail the disputative dilemma,
Don't limit yourself,
You will get the unfeigned call only in desperation,
The fearless plod on unheeding,
The heart calls to mind and holds you back and warns
you of uncertainties that lie ahead,
Don't get pulled into the apparent glitters,
Let your soul strive systematic darkness,
Soar with zeal abundance,
Time is sorrowful as well as life-affirming.

Despicable Denial

Who will ever understand?
That it's a memory she carries,
A moment she's awaited all year,
A moment she wished to relive the most.

Life truly stings when denial takes hold,
All those memories flood her mind,
All those playful moments break down,
All that was planned remains unchanged.

Old is still gold; the trace of time smiles,
As bursts of laughter fill the air,
Like glowing, remarkable gems,
The enlightened craving unforgettable delicacies,
Curing, like sudden, curable remedies.

An atypical accusation—unwilling to fade,
Invariably savoring the artful deception,
Not yet ready to soften the ravenous, dreary journey,
A twisted quandary dances against the once-sharp
reflection.

The ghost of the past caught in the fire—anticipating
joy,
Gazes at the silent feud over his possessions.
Poor child, ineffectually trying to avoid the conflict,
As ominous black clouds gather in heavy crowds.

When will they understand?
It's not a lie, for heaven's sake.
When will the trust be restored in those eyes?
When will they ever let her breathe again?

Tired of hedging their bets, they banished her,
Her pleas vanished, swallowed by darkness,
Silence understood every word she spoke,
The loner found solace in the ghost of memories,
A reflection that haunted every thought.

Her rare world, quiet and distinct,
Full of dreams yet to be realized,
She soon became a hawk with velvet claws.

The Beauty of Acceptance

If you love someone, embrace their soul,
Every imperfection makes them whole.
No one is flawless, none without stain,
But beauty lies in what they contain.

Love not your shadow within their light,
But the truth of them, both wrong and right.
For love is blind, a boundless grace,
It sees the heart, not just the face.

Perfection is woven with threads of flaws,
Love stands pure, without pause.
A masterpiece of imperfections combined,
A divine gift to humankind.

Almighty loves us, despite our fall,
Granting us mercy, forgiving it all.
He never demands we conform to His way,
So why should we shape others like clay?

There's beauty in those who remain true,
In their choices, in all they do.
Judge not, for sin takes different guise,
Only time reveals where goodness lies.

So, love openly, let joy take flight,
Smile brighter, live in the light.
For life's too brief to live in disdain,
Let love and kindness be your domain.

Indescribable Feeling

That moment when words slip away,
Alone, yet embracing the bliss of solitude,
Eyes blink, surprised, as a weight settles in the chest,
A quiet rhythm that pulses with a steady beat.
The stomach growls, restless with hunger.

Observation sharpens,
Like the ticking of a clock—punctual and accurate,
Noticing even the gradual shake of the curtain,
Hearing the subtle sounds that often go unheard.

Mind and heart flutter; the chest feels empty,
A dumbfounded smile forms, then fades,
Followed by a quiet whisper of warning:
"Shhh," the heart says, asking for calm.

The unease lingers, unresolved,
The mind stirs with thoughts that won't settle,
Tension builds, a soft pressure,
Words of frustration slip out unbidden.

She presses against the wall, seeking solace in its cold
embrace,
Tears at the tangled thoughts—
But still, that restlessness remains,
Lingering like a whisper.

That moment when you are caught in stillness,
With nothing but quiet thoughts swirling around.

Disguised Fluke

Who will ever decipher?
The summer heart, throbbing in her throat,
Like a stone flowing in a riverbed,
Enduring without complaint.

That pleasurable pain, the gloomiest ever,
Creates an ambiance, utterly standstill,
She screams, whining,
But no one is there for comfort.

And there she lies awake,
An insomniac once more,
Awake in the darkness of her sin,
With the innocent demons of her own.

The dejection of murderous bereavement,
The affliction of trauma,
So devastated, so woe-begone,
Like a grey area.

Gone wild in the memory,
She ultimately turns her back,
Glad to see the end of that treacherous recollection of
murder,
Of a man who made her life hell.

Ultimately, after years, she recovered herself,
She finds euphoria,
Her heart satisfied with the bliss of success,
Knocking on her doorstep, infinite.

Nostalgic Bijou

The cold breeze blew my hair,
I could not feel the air,
Rushing hard against my face,
Busy winning the lost race.

Struggling to ace a lost battle,
Preparing to face a good fight,
My feet leave marks,
Not easy for someone to fit in.

A path few of us would choose,
Vanishes before someone could park in,
Cold water strokes as if it had nothing to lose,
Ecstatic memories reveal my sins.

As sweet as apple pie,
Memories of the drowning sky,
I could see angels; I could hear my past,
It all just ran through me, neither slow nor fast.

I lost my way into an extinct kingdom,
The presence of freedom filled my lacerations,
Adulthood all new; climbing the steps of wisdom,
Seemed as if I was introduced to a whole new globe
of nations.

Abrupt prick awakened me,
Harsh reality saddened me,
And then the heart of me weeps
Craving for the gem-the days of glory,
But unwillingly accepts the truth and continues its
fragile story.

Old War Wounds

Moonlight embellishing the old war wounds that
cheapens,
Ached by the darkness in the cold-dry sound that
deepens,
Red crucifix dulled since years ultimately weakens,
Insomnia preached again by those intolerable reasons,
Everyone else had slept after eons,
Possessed by his own demons,
Silence was his constant companion for all seasons,
Somewhat paralyzed, he was occupied by disastrous
illusions,
One after the other in furious elisions,
Harsh lullabies were heard from painful disillusions,
Memories stung him in disguised perfections,
Guilt felt too extreme in outrageous accretion,
Darkness seemed familiar in its purest completion,
He loved her enough to let her go with his
prepossessing lesions,
Demons muttered a few indecipherable words
captivated by Legion,
Ambience trapped in trepidation,
A mystery for generations,
Abrupt smirk frightened the ghost in horrification,
Dissolved in the disguised wickedness of fake
fascination,
Karma's war was miraculous, like fire in a diamond.

The Beyond

Sacrifice is compulsory,
Dink your tears and bring up your smiles,
Leave unnecessary toils and prostrate,
Life in this world does not go on forever,
It's short and sweet, meant to be treasured,
Choose the path of scorching deserts and fight your
devils,
Seek refuge in the Lord, not people,
These days will drift away like clouds, so make good
deeds your constant companion,
We all live in an illusion life; tomorrow is not
guaranteed,
Don't forget the enemy of this life; face it with purity,
Let your mortal be inhabited by the purest of the
immortal,
For the sinner shall taste the fire indeed,
Limbs torn apart by the wrath, you will see.

The Prayer of Innocence Refine

What do you gain in Salah,
Unless you bow in Sujood?
The remembrance of the Creator
Makes me unworthy of the being I am.

The remembrance of my idol
Disappoints me for not following his teachings,
The lighthouse of guidance I failed to heed.
Contemplating my life, I am astonished by my faith,
Accepting my destiny, yet my sins disappoint me.

Repentance, proven by the blues,
A guilt trip that degrades the psyche,
Regret for not being righteous in His book,
Throes of remorse spill like blood in a carcass.

Reflecting on present blessings,
I forget the past,
While 'Nur' enlightens the immortal soul.
Numerous wonders appear before my eyes,
Agape awakens the inner ego,

The hunger for materialism dies,
Awakening the never-ending spark!
God knows the heart and searches the motives,
The world is the test, and Jannah is the goal—
For you cannot serve both God and mammon.

Time is Precious

Gazing at the nature, I dive into the galaxies,
My feet sank in the sand as the cold water brought
peace.
I flew to an extinct kingdom at the count of three,
Where I hear a voice, very atypical and free.

"Time am I; grasp me in every spot,
For thy Lord entrusted me with the forgotten,
contemporary, and the fate you keep.
Catch hold of me as I run out, of course,
Stepping soundlessly like a newborn baby.

I am not a maelstrom; behold me!
You can find me in the morning sun and dive with
me in the ink-black way."

Woken up by the gale, harsh reality saddens me.

Time is a powerful gem!
A running opportunity for the wilted stems.
Possess it, for it flies quick; you will soon be a flicker
in a wall of bricks.

Mini seconds bind the dark clouds to the vibrant
skies,
So, avail yourself of your gold like a mother caring for
a child.
Get hold of this ruby, for it never comes to a halt,
For time, once out of hand, it is all your fault.

Be a diligent mortal that never sleeps,
As ominous as the time that creeps up,
Within his bosom shall you sleep,
So, make a name before you weep.

Time is a neutral path to attend; it has neither rivals
nor friends.
Time is precious; I should say, a muscular invocation
as polished as a glace.

The pathway of time is somewhat distinct,
Our years flow as the runnel slips away,
This root of Earth vanishes in a blink,
Guiding the cunning through the darkest way.

A difficult challenge, time is!
Try it- I dare you!
It will set you in a mystified test,
Where success gifted by Him knocks on your door in
a minuscule mile.

Ominous Demons

You came in when everyone left,
You were a rainbow in my solitude,
A beam that gleamed in the ink-black way,
My soul ultimately satisfied—drops after drops,
Heart playful at the sight of rain,
Hearing the drops clapping, watching the leaves
dance.

Your hand reinvigorated my soul,
Like those wilted plants freshened as their roots
drank near.
The darkness was gone,
A wondrous immortal filled in.
The moon dived into the black blanket,
Trust vanished the doubtful bitterness.

I hope the Sun shines bright,
Positive belief is the most essential.
Kindred spirits like you are rare,
Our souls are meant to bind.

Goosebumps of the Soul

The sound of rain came like lively guffaws,
So ecstatic, it almost made me forget everything.
How wonderful it was—
The falling crystals brought cheers and brilliant luck.

Each drop led to a mysterious world,
Concealing untold secrets beneath its veil.
The universe united in one color—
Greenery embellished the joy brought down.

Down, in the language of the Almighty,
Cars vanished like bullets in the ever-growing fog.
Visions went blind, yet fear did not touch me,
For God's eye watched, surrounded by His
unspeakable guards.

I saw bushes jumping, trees dancing,
Each move fueled by the green elixir.
Racing like jets, one after the other,
I let the drops bounce off my face, some dissolving in
the air.

A pleasant feeling, soothing and pure.
As I made my way home, I heard constant clashes,
Unparalleled to the hum of the engine.
My conscience refused to move ahead,
Ears dying to hear the mysteries waiting.

My soul, never so alive,
Breaking the rules, I felt free, I felt capable.
My heart felt like a bird freed from its cage.
Orange lights faded, unfamiliar as they hid in the
glitters,
Deception blacked out; love illuminated perception.

I felt so deep, so comfortable for the first time—
Not possessed, but alive,
Love danced lively, spreading its charm,
Soothing my inner self with every beat.

Heart at ease, I watched nature's show,
Enjoying every moment to the fullest.
Heat poured inside but could not prevail
Over the cold chills, I felt outside.

The weather, so pleasant, sent shivers down my
spine,
Goosebumps rising in the best possible way.
Undefinable, it presented agape in its purest form.
Birds sang, humans soared like kites.

The aura was the complete opposite,
I saw a different version of this world.
Was it truly calm,
Or just harsh reality disguised?

Absolutely still, I watched the gleaming show,
Not wishing it to end with every elixir that fell.

Forlorn

Scurrying in the deepest and the darkest of her soul,
She drowned in the never-ending pool of
impossibility,
The path that made her forget.
Forget how it was to be bitten by the sharks or chased
by the wild natives,
A home where she loved until she couldn't anymore,
A home where she treasured him, not ready to lose,
Now there she lays as a tree losing her essential,
Like the sunlight, she was filled with false magical
alarms,
Lights dimmed, fixated on the shadow that
diminished,
She could not sway back and forth between the lonely
sunshine and the ecstatic darkness,
She was lost like an infant in a stream of throng.

Her Exquisite Light

Skull as soft as a bird,
Eyes like almonds, round like a bottle lid,
So adorable and so idyllic, smile unmatchable,
Frantic hikes, laconic and astute,
Lively cheers burst forth,
So indecipherable yet so fulfilling,
Every nook and corner dance in the spotlight.

A single glance enriches the seed in the worn-out earth;
The God's gift brought numerous blessings,
Making a difference in the locked faiths;
Vanishing pain abruptly as rain throws a blanket of green elixir;
Her existence effective as the nuclear explosion;
The doll ignited flames against fiends so fragile and delicate,
An exquisite cameo amidst judgmental beauty.

Sunshine and Shadows

Wait for the sunshine; it never announces its arrival.
The mechanism of hope is somewhat distinct.
Nothing in life comes without hard work;
A handful of success comes after a bucket of failures.
Experts are born after tons of practice.
Monuments are noticed as they withstand numerous
adverse trials.
Beautiful places are visited after ages of refinement.
Seeds grow in their own idyllic way, distinct from the
mechanized world.
Everyone is unknown when they step into the world.
The hope recipe is quite tough to follow:
A portion of hard work, with a dash of success,
A tablet of hope and sprinkles of failure,
Mixed in the ocean of self-confidence.
Such a meal will do it all, for hope should never die.
A seed that grows into a tree of hard work,
Leaves dance in endless lullabies of comfort, infinite
green!

Journey of Perfection

Driving through the curves, my heart caught in my
throat,
Music poured from the open windows,
An aura raucous, lights blazing bright.
The beauty overwhelming, enriched, yet haunting.

Greenery so absorbing, I longed to stay,
People of every race—familiar, yet strange.
The place so exciting, I sold my heart,
Curves leading to skies, mist welcoming me in.

Each turn held a mystery,
Drizzles dancing in the twilight,
Monkeys, cows, birds of every kind—
Each here, with its own reason for being.

The view sent signals, connecting with my heart,
Filling my soul with countless paintings.
So welcoming, devoted, and admiring,
The vision entered deep, beyond the doorsteps of
sight.

The guards stood in their green army suits,
Squinting when headlights shone upon them.
Nature played its jazz, an ancient feat,
Talent displayed like books in a well-kept library.

Mountain's irregular, yet geometrically perfect,
So tall, so infinite, towering above.
Eyeballs amazed at the unblemished beauty,
Tears rushed out from the perfection that gripped my
soul.

The dauntless welcomed me into this never-ending
journey,
Where escape was but a distant dream.
I stepped on clouds, drifting away,
To the land of the unknown.

I allowed myself to get wet in purity,
Blessings showered upon me like rain.
I knocked on His door and found the reason for my
existence—
As vital as water in a drought, food in famine.

For the first time, darkness felt like a bed of flowers,
The sun said its last goodbye,
Drowned in the river of dark eternity,
Sending fragrance of radio waves in good riddance.

I smelt the figments of danger high above,
Followed by the stigma of expected hopes and
excitement.
Everyone's existence is important—
Never lose hope.

We are all here for a reason.
Find your purpose,
And launch like a rocket into the newborn dawn.

Nostalgia in the Dark

Little ones, as brave as lions,
Adults, as skilled as expert pickpockets.
The harsh life of damp, wet sand pricks at me,
Roads illuminated by headlights alone.

A black blanket with a pearl head wraps around me,
Playing hide and seek with its team of fireflies.
Exodus stares as if they've never witnessed such
personality.

Lowering my gaze, I wait for my destination to hurry,
Earth so absorbed in darkness, unfriendly.
Eyes as large as stars,
Squinting the universe down to the size of a dot.

Eyes barely spotting the path,
The unfamiliar darkness haunts me,
My soul nostalgic for its comfort zone.

Echoes and Strength

Remembering him comes with the clash of galaxies,
Remembering him comes with the pull of waves.
Remembering him approaches me with mysteries
unmatched.

Remembering him also brings positive vibes,
Remembering him fuels my determination,
Remembering him challenges me,
Remembering him empowers me with strength.

Let him drown in the endless mist—
Beautiful, yet dangerous.

Don't let your emotions stray from your current path.
Be strong. Face hardships, even when it feels
impossible.
For those who put you down aren't worth your tears.
Instead, find confidence in who you are.

Know yourself and embrace what suits you.
Misfortune is always followed by fortune,
For that is the hidden of life—
Infinite, mysterious, and waiting to unfold.

The Light Within

Above the horizon, I see the sun rising,
Clouds like cotton drift through a velvet sky.
How beautiful the view, so full of splendor,
Mesmerizing, with a touch of ardor.

The orangish glow lights the land once dim,
Gloom fades, replaced by a tranquil hymn.
Fresh and breathtaking, it calls me to follow,
A path once hidden in the shadows of sorrow.

My heart awakens, a spark is reborn,
Finding joy in wonders so finely adorned —
Tiny beauties shining bright in the dark,
Like a "jugnoo," igniting life's quiet spark.

A new self emerges, unseen before,
Love reveals its truths, an infinite lore.
For those who know it, love never fades,
And knowledge, once gained, never decays.

The Veins of Stone

Mountains face the blue, velvety companion,
Trees agonize like magnetars, united in their
persistence.
I see cows, and in their eyes, they feast on pies.
Each one with their own destination,
A sense of freedom in every glance, yet trapped in
trepidation.

Driving roughly over the road without a trace of
guilt,
A man of stone, his rock with veins, a colt with
untamed will.
Fixated eyes of strange innocence,
Smirks caught in the golden steps of sunshine, built in
weirdness.

Like seaweed swaying back and forth with the waves,
Channels of shockwaves scatter my thoughts like
fallen leaves.
The place silenced by massive sacrifices,
The place silenced by patience unwanted, lingering.

Unable to do anything, my heart longs to help every
wanderer,
Yet it vanishes, as if by the quick trick of a magician.
Gloomily, I look ahead and step away,
For dreams are hardly ever meant to be fulfilled.

Whispers Under Moonlight

Green moonlight, as beautiful as the night sky,
Fireflies like traffic lights gently illuminating the
smooth, symmetrical outline.
Caterpillars sing rhythmically, swaying back and
forth,
Enthusiastic rhymes embrace me; my stomach squints
with roars of laughter.

Conversations send chills down the spine;
Abrupt enthusiasm sways it all away.
Eyes gleam in triumph, making shapes with the dots,
A mind finally happy after aeons, good cheers
wrapping my heart.

A cart under the influence of pomegranates,
Body shivering yet carefree,
Limbs strongly refuse to hide.

Aphids like soldiers marching,
Plant bugs flying frantically.
Lying on the charpoy,
Confidently facing the unfamiliar shapes drawn in
black ink.

The whole night listening to the mighty talkers,
Mesmerizing sunrise paints the sky with captivating
shades,
Soon tending to the excited souls.

The Path to Extraordinary

How many times do we dream and create,
Pursuing the extraordinary, defying our fate?
How often do we toil with hearts so true,
Only to face failure, with critics in view?

For nothing in life is handed with ease,
Success demands effort, no shortcuts to seize.
Failure through effort is a lesson, a guide,
But failure from neglect is where faults reside.

Focus on growth, let your spirit ascend,
Don't waste time in criticism that leads to no end.
Life offers no gifts with an open hand,
Opportunities bloom where you choose to stand.

Face negativity with grace; don't let it invade,
Their aim is to dim you—don't let light fade.
Surrender to positivity; let it fill your core,
With perseverance, you'll rise and soar.

A Midnight Awakening

Midnight arrives, my soul begins to ache,
Yearning for something I cannot awake.
Annoyance, aggression, emotions entwined,
A restless chaos consumes my mind.

Then I see a shadow, mysterious, divine,
A call so alluring, a presence to confine.
Impatient yet calm, dangerous yet safe,
Frightened yet trusting in its gentle embrace.

Suddenly, I vanish, a world unfolds,
Where my art of own age quietly takes hold.
White trails glisten on the blackened sand,
Guiding me softly, like a soothing hand.

A pull draws me into a wondrous haze,
With mirrored people and trees ablaze.
Orange and red, their leaves alight,
Contributing purity to the aura's delight.

I feel so unburdened, loved, and free,
Ecstatic and light in this reverie.
Yet, reality strikes, harsh and unkind,
An angel awakens me, her voice refined.

So, refreshing, so calm, she quells the storm,
A soothing presence, tender and warm.
Her whispers shield the innocent shores,
Where raging tempests return no more.

Indelible Moments

My lips curve into an unshaken twinkle, enduring the
pain that pulses within,
As I reminisce the times we've shared, a solace
against the world's din.
The world, lost in time, feels off-track and numb,
As my orison, dispatched to the heavens, helplessly
plummets down.

Whenever I steal moments to think of you,
My heart lights up, finding the lost soul anew.
In your eyes, I long to drift into endless sleep,
In your heart, I wish for my cherished memories to
keep.

You are my treasure, the most precious one,
For your love, my heart bows where victories are
won.
Oh, how much I love you—my wealth, my fate,
It's a gush of fluke that brought you through my gate.

You are my destiny, the fulfillment of my desires,
Since I found you, my world burns with radiant fires.
Don't drift away, stay close to my heart,
Wrap your hands around it; never let us part.

Today, as I remember those golden times,
The heartache fades, replaced by celestial chimes.
My mind soars like a colorful kite in the sky,
Should I seek answers or let the wonder fly?

Your fragrance rests deeply within my chest,
Your head, a gem on my shoulder, perfectly blessed.
Come, merge into my silhouette, day and night,
Don't vanish like laughter on a cold wind's flight.

When I see those idyllic landscapes—pure finesse,
They soothe the aching loneliness my heart possesses.
Yet, when those diamonds are missed, their glow is
gone,
The soul dances aimlessly in a smog that lingers on.

The Power of a Smile

Smile as the sun rises,
Smile more as the sun sets.
Smile among the dancing hearts,
Smile more among the wilted flowers.

Smile for a wicked diplomat,
Smile more for a clean-hearted gem.
Smile when you have the world in your fist,
Smile more when you don't own a penny.

Smile when you touch the highest skies,
Smile more when you're lost in the thickest dust.
Smile under the heavy heap of stones,
Smile more when you're being crushed underfoot.

Smile gently to color your surroundings,
Smile more when your heart denies the need.
Smile among the praising applauds,
Smile more when they put you down.

Smile among your usual pals,
Smile more amidst your enemies.
Smile forever, for it's a sunnah,
The moon chases behind bright, smiling faces.

Fading Harmony

Watching the birds fly by,
I vanished into a new globe passing by.
The sunlight colored the sky in hues so bright,
Brightening the landscapes, gracing the newborn's
face with delight.

Music danced out of the open windows,
While rushing horns stood still, stiff as arrows.
The cold breeze felt soothing, so fulfilling,
Its harmonic beauty carried me into a trance so
thrilling.

For a moment, everything seemed within my grasp,
But the beat awakened my soul, revealing an empty
clasp.
Suddenly, nothing was mine, and all felt astray,
As the dominating beauty led me down an agonizing
way.

My essentials waned, dissolving like sand in the air,
Leaving behind traces of disappointment and despair.
Nature bears the brunt of ruthless greed,
Each harsh step drops its rhythm, a somber deed.

The heart sinks deep at the sight of blackened blooms,
The ocean dense with chaos, grease, and doom.
Once-vibrant life now faces extinction's sting,
Innocent breeds lost, victims of humankind's
reckoning.

Artificial beauty chokes, hard to inhale,
An aura, once a shield, now tips the scale.
Be the savior of your wealth, for it is your bulwark,
For a mistake made once is inevitable;
Twice, it becomes a choice.

This Time

Eyes cried till they bled.
This time, you returned, yet why did my ego weep?
My soul fed on love,
The memories stung, the poison climbed gradually.
I stood still,
My limbs—smashing, roaring relentlessly.
This time, it was distinct.
This time, love was a deadly enemy.
This time, I couldn't feel your love.
This time, I stood ice cold.

When Shadows Fall

The guffaws, so remarkable,
The talks—never-ending,
Eyes gleamed with love,
The world danced around me.
Then your shadow crept,
I could smell the fear,
I could feel the silence screaming,
I withstood the terrific; it was no small thing.
I could see your eyes cast a spell,
I could not feel your heart beating against me,
I could feel your ice-cold waves,
I could see our souls wilting,
I could see our hands falling apart,
I watched you walk away.

Shadows of a Lost Soul

Deep beneath the oceans, above the skies,
The shore swarmed with an aggressive horde of
fireflies.
The frequency of waves pulled me astray,
Through distinct waterways, I drifted away.
I am but a shadow that rests and roams,
A fifty-year-old skeleton, burdened, alone.

In the mountain streams, I wish to paddle,
But my limbs grow weary, my mind begins to
scrabble.
An old soul lost in offensive trivialities,
And harmless convivialities.

Thoughts and reflections—funny yet poignant,
Personal yet universal, confusing yet
comprehensible—
They flow through me in a style so sensible.

An unbelievable trace leads to a haunting future,
Where goosebumps rise as genocides feed the
vulture.
Giant snakes poison the innocent's veins,
Cold metal dissolves into the blood at a rate
unrestrained.

Dauntless laughter fades, leaving a memorable
vestige,
Hatred masked by fake smiles and counterfeit
leverage.
The ambiance—atypical, defunct—
Where souls ascend with heartbreaking adieus.

Together, We Fly

Thinking of us separating scares me,
Frightens me a lot.
My soul becomes out of hand.
I have to constantly reassure myself that you are with
me.
When our palms fit so perfectly, my heart dives into
peace.
Your guffaws are so harmonic;
My grief-stricken demon dances carelessly.
The angelic perfumes fill my wounds and make me
unconscious of the being I am.
My conscience turns crazy.
You are my comfort zone.
Your sight makes my day.
Forgetting you is surely an impossible battle,
Unless on purpose!
You reside within me.
Your scent flows through me.
You and I, together, we can fly through galaxies.
Together, we can write our chapters in the night sky.
Together, we can talk to the moon about lifelong
melodies.
Together, our love will be untainted from the
ominous demons.

The Pencil and the Sapling

Do not be like an arch in practice,
Bear a clear and distinct target,
Select your area of operation,
Hit abrupt to the point.
Be like an ordinary pencil,
Symbolic of life's trials and triumphs,
Totes open to love, even if others hurt.
Wake up and smell the coffee!
Things have changed!
The saplings have become destructive trees,
Love, sweet love, is thought a crime.

The Journey of Life

Life is rarely fair,
Like steel, it never demolishes,
Or, like a thin branch, it breaks in seconds.

Bad experiences creep like an ominous shadow.
Good times elevate you like a vibrant kite in
darkness.

Travel on the moon and fall among the stars,
Spread your wings and let the stones make you soar.

Take it as the only first chance,
Stay wild as thoughts and free like a feather.

Live in the caves but leave remarkable traits,
Do not get carried away by this sweet, sweet breeze!

You carry life in your hands,
Let it go and live the darkest luck,
Treasure it and enjoy the eternal soothing.

Promises Meant to be Broken

Sitting out there, staring at the moon, I miss again.
After all that's happened between us,
Why does a part of me still long for you?
I am a wreck—emotionally and mentally.

My palms ache,
My heart feels heavy.
I wish you were here.
But you are not.

I'm struggling, and you're moving on.
Every morning, I hope we'll meet again,
But reality pulls me back, tearing at my peace.
Your presence lingers in my mind.

I want to be there for you,
To ease your pain.
I hope for warmth in my life,
Filled with happiness, like it once was.

You left, saying promises are meant to be broken.
That was then, and my feelings for you are still
strong,
But I'll hold back because promises are meant to be
broken.

The Weight of Change

Why do I feel so heavy?
My heart feels like cold metal.
Why can't I feel the breeze?
My mind is drowned in stress.
Why can't I laugh freely?
My soul feels dark and distant.
Why have I lost my voice?
My words spill out like bullets.
Why am I so isolated?
My silence stretches for miles.
How did I become so sure?
I've welcomed demons as companions.
Why am I so numb?
I've lost the person I once knew.

The Paradox of Love

This sea of thoughts is so depressing,
It carries me to the treacherous depth, tied in the
knots,
How badly it wraps around me
So tightly! I can't even breathe.

Oh, sweet love, why do you do this?
Oh, sweet love, why are you so harsh?
Oh, sweet love, why are you easy?
Oh, sweet love, stop camouflaging your face.

Love, love, love- a murderous bite!
Separate your reflection and follow its traits,
To a world very strange,
Where I hope love, sweet love, truly tastes like honey.

Lost and Unfound

Maybe I was wrong. Maybe I wasn't.
Noticing the change, I simply switched off.
I became my own enemy in the sparkling abyss.
I saw my angels fading,
My hero walking away.
All I could do was watch them leave.

The poison I inhaled numbed me,
As their shadows faded,
My soul craved their presence,
But my limbs were paralyzed, too numb to move.

It wasn't in my hands—it was destined.
Tears streamed from my reddened eyes,
I felt like someone had punched me in the soul.
I hid when I couldn't,
I endured the thorns when I couldn't,
I smiled when I couldn't.

First, I lost my heart,
Then, I lost my mind.
I was lost.
Was sleep my only refuge? At least I could escape for
a while.

When I woke and stared at my reflection,
I saw a dull, lost doll—heartlessly beaten.
The doll was lost.
I don't know where, but she was.

I could hear my hero and angel knocking.
Maybe family were the ones who came looking,
When I was lost,
But I chose to ignore,
Chose to walk away,
Because sometimes, the most beautiful parts of life
Can only be found by getting lost.

The Warrior's Heart

The wheezing, so thoughtful, walks in my senses,
Where the thrills, so dead, are soon conquered
By the thought that enhances;
That girl within, sweetened by lullabies.

She sits on a lonely street,
A place with no beginning.
She walks to deadly rhythms,
Pretending it's her first-ever tweet.

Her world, conquered by a black blanket,
Enjoyed ecstatically by her broken heart.
Her world, perfected with her first play of trumpet,
Enjoyed deeply by her only heart.

She tries to run miles without leaving a trace,
She tries to hide where I can't feel her.
She tries to stay quiet, so I won't blame her,
She tries to make up for her mistakes in the prison.

The teachable spirit endures a lot,
The humble spirit learns a lot.

This warrior will surely win her battles,
This warrior will surely overcome the adversities.

She shuts off as the wheezing closes.

Who is She?

Letting the world suck me in,
Into the deepest of its fears,
Where I see that girl losing herself,
Yet also living her life.
Who is she?
Who is she?
Who is she?

The darkest of her demons?
The humblest of her angels?
The fairest of her heart?
The bravest of her mind?
Who is she?
Who is she?
Who is she?

She is just a girl coping with her life,
She is just a girl trying her best to climb…
The deepest of the lacuna.

The Battle of Life

Life is not easy.
When it's going well,
Know it will knock you down.
When it's going rough,
Know it will lift you up.

Deal with circumstances as if they are your worst
enemies.
Learn to live with them in one house.
Learn to face them harshly, like the wind gushing
through your face.
Learn to prevail over them, like an open-mouthed
battle abruptly won.

Meant to Be?

Once in a lifetime,
We were meant to be,
In some circumstances,
But never ought to be.

In dreams, we met,
We traveled together on the lyrics we wept.
How can I lose you,
In relationships never meant to be?

Those three words creep on me like ominous
shadows.
I can't let you hold my hand,
I will break even more.
True love is found in the heavens,
Where we are meant to be,
Not in this disastrous pity,
Where our souls become strangers before we even
meet.

Whispers of the Heart

Funny, what an obsession can do,
A whispered warning: don't fall through.
Love is a game, a treacherous art,
Yet trust remains the king of hearts.

A portent of death—it lingers near,
What is love without trust sincere?
What is trust without love's embrace?
I don't even know where to place this space.

You can't truly fix a broken heart,
I long to drive, to tear apart.
To vanish in the thick black air,
Where ghosts of terrors freely stare.

I want to run through the blank unknown,
To absorb the light, let it make me whole.
To drink the elixir that rains from above,
To feel my soul bleed, yet rise in love.

I'll watch myself break, then rebuild anew,
Heal my wounds, find skies to pursue.
I'll fly in ecstasy, unbound, untamed,
But still, this space between us is framed.

My love for you, like the steadfast moon,
You may not always see me soon.
Yet even unseen, I'm always there,
A quiet presence in the evening air.

The Ghost of You

Why do I even think of you?
I've learned to live half-alive,
To exist among my own friends.
I want to forget you.
I refuse to waste my tears,
To doubt myself anymore.

Don't come back—
You'll tear me apart even more.
Don't come back at all!

I can't take another step toward you.
You lost the spark,
That once ignited me to my fullest.

Stop haunting my dreams.
Stop ruining my present.

I've finally pieced myself together.
It took so long to feel alright.

Now,
Let me live.
Let me live.
Let me live.

You are not my ghost anymore.

The Glamorous Game of Life

Have you ever found yourself willing to do
everything for someone,
Only to face the cold indifference of their back?
Never trade your self-worth for someone
Who doesn't care enough to make you smile,
Who doesn't value your respect.

People come and go; they rarely stay.
The ones who remain are those who strive to be with
you,
Who put effort into keeping you happy,
Who respect you as deeply as you respect them.

Never sell yourself short.
Never let yourself be just an option.
Human nature is such—chasing after stones,
Discarding the diamonds.
They believe you'll always return—
So don't. Let them feel your absence,
Let them realize your worth.

Once you've moved forward,
Leave the past behind.
In a world built of bricks,
Climbing the ladder of success means;
There will always be hands trying to pull you down.
After all, who wants to see someone else rise
When they're stuck?
The devils are never idle.

Open your eyes.
Tie your heart and soul to Him,
For your Lord is the Most Merciful.
True love—agape—is a warm breeze
That uplifts and shapes your spirit.

Create your own unique mark on this world.
A true friend can be closer than family,
But beware—a deadly enemy
Can stand even closer than your truest friend.

Be wise.
Life is no ready-made garment,
No pre-cut pattern.
It is a game—a glamorously horrific game—
And you are both its player and its prize.

The Bond That Shines

Demons are known to never sleep,
As ominous as time, that silently creeps.
Souls lost in a dim abyss,
Yet saved by each other's faith and bliss.

Amid scattered seeds, they stand in grace,
Binding magically, no need for space.
Together, they explore their deepest gems,
Once concealed from the outside realm.

Pinky promises, like Tinker Bell's spell,
Unbreakable, timeless stories to tell.
Laughter that soars and touches the skies,
Warm hugs that soothe where solace lies.

Hand in hand, they face the snakes,
Waging battles with smiles that don't break.
How brightly they glow in the darkest night,
Even as evil eyes follow each step with spite.

Friendship so true, an invocation divine,
Superficial codes—indecipherable, infinite.
Shoulder to shoulder, their spirits alight,
Together, they'll shine, a breathtaking sight.

The Abyss Within

The memories devoured me, tearing hope apart,
Limb by limb—smashing my bones to shards.
I became blank, a hollow shell,
My soul ablaze with unrelenting rage.

Darkness I was, and darkness I became.
How I wish I had never fallen.

Carried away by the merciless tides,
My tears, like anchors,
Dragged me deep into a boundless pool of
impossibility.

Didn't you hear me scream?
Or did you simply choose to ignore?

Colorful Confusion

I am tired.
Tired of the melodrama.
Feuds with my own demons have crossed their limits.
I am done—ultimately done.

I will shine like fireflies,
Beautifying my darkness in my own way.
I don't need you.
I don't love you anymore.

I will be my own helping hand.
The cold, lonely forest inside me,
And those insidious clouds,
Are my worst enemies.

Within me, you will find a glamorous beam,
Gleaming with the satisfaction of acceptance.
But you will also be frightened
By the concealed, dangerous ink-black night,
Where my fairies and fiends struggle in turmoil.

My soul is lost,
Yet I am a colorful landscape,
Vibrantly alive.

I am a solved puzzle,
But also a perplexing nightmare,
As haunting as a prison.
I am as deep as the ocean's depth,
And as beautifully open as a waterfall.

I am cold-hearted,
But I melt instantly.
Still, I am just a normal girl.

Malignant Perfidy

She howled like a wolf as her past drew near,
Its claws raked memories she held dear.
Shattered like glass, her heart did cry,
As if thunder had struck from a darkened sky.

She recalled her days, once bright, serene,
When love adorned her world, pristine.
His gaze once gleamed with promises sweet,
Now shadows replaced where their hearts would meet.

"How could he do this?" her whispers pled,
As tears fell fast from eyes that bled.
Her pale face bore the scars of despair,
A soul unraveling beyond repair.

In trembling breaths, she murmured low,
Words that only the winds would know.
Pain coursed through her like an endless tide,
Her anguish no longer could she hide.

She lay still beneath the moonlit glow,
As crimson rivers began to flow.
Yet in her torment, a strange peace grew,
For the hurt of her past, she at last withdrew.

Her eyes closed softly; her lips formed a prayer,
"Why did he leave me? Was he ever there?"
Like a crumpled page from a tale forgot,
She rested where the world could hurt her not.

Under the stars, her spirit took flight,
A ghostly child through galaxies bright.
Bound to the heavens, she sought her peace,
Where pain and betrayal would finally cease.

Fragments of a Faded Dream

She lingered on days when a smile so bright
Could fill her soul with endless light.
One name alone had brought her peace,
Turning loneliness into sweet release.

But now that ship has sailed away,
And love became a fleeting play.
Those midnight talks, those whispered lies,
Now linger as shadows beneath the skies.

The reel of memories spun through her mind,
A movie of dreams left far behind.
Insomnia gripped her through the night,
Yet she sought to recall what once felt right.

"People come and go," she softly sighed,
A truth she once had cast aside.
Regret lingered where hope had been,
For love, she'd thought, would never dim.

How cleverly played, the game so sly,
The memories tore, yet she questioned, "Why?"
Her soul was stabbed by conscience keen,
A world now broken, no longer serene.

Yet within moments, her lips found grace,
A fragile smile lit her face.
Tears that fell spoke pain she bore,
But resolve arose to heal once more.

Her spirit rested, calm, and still,
A quiet strength replaced the thrill.
With scars that marked where love once stayed,
She moved ahead, unafraid.

Luminescence of the Shadows

Walking in darkness, I come to know my fate—
Where the impossible turns possible, and the possible
escapes.
An ocean of lava beneath my feet, a galaxy of stars
above,
I marvel at nature's beauty in the night, dark yet
deeply profound.

I absorb the shadows like a sponge, never sated,
Feeding my soul with the quiet strength of positivity.
Darkness, sometimes dreadful and woebegone,
Other times, idyllic, outrageously glamorous, drawn.

Conceiving angels, I face my vulnerable reflection—
Aggressive, splintered into moonlit shards.
They shine like insignificant diamonds,
Drifting in malignant elixirs, abruptly crossing His
path.
For the Lord is bountiful—The Merciful, The
Gracious,
His endless love, incomparable and vast.

A path once barren of solace now glows with
soothing radiance,
Where misfortune seemed eternal, now disguised
blessings bloom.
The Almighty's grace changes all.

With this realization, lethargic eyes open wide in
submission.
The scaphoid bone aches, but the prostration persists.
A heart sinks in repentance,
Awake to the countless favors of His hand.

It is better to seek refuge in the Lord than in man,
For His mercy is a light eternal, a guidance without
end.

Threads of Obsession,

Paths of Love

A Short Story

"We are as distinct as a deer is from a lion," he said. He didn't want to be the destroyer of her life. Yet, every time they met, he saw a new version of her—a different spark that made his eyes brighten, revealing his love without words.

Her cheeks would flush, and her soft pink slips faltered, leaving her speechless—a language of love only they could understand. She found her world in him, exploring galaxies simply by being nearby. Her once-dark lost soul now burned with fire, not light, ignited by his presence.

Little did she know, her love had grown into an obsession—not a partnership. This terrified him. Obsession became the shark among innocent dolphins, devouring them one by one. Like fire consuming paper, it spiraled into a storm with silken reins—beautiful, yet uncontrollable.

The purity of their bond, once as flawless as diamonds, had turned as insidious as rocks pulsing with veins. She couldn't bear the weight of her obsession as it vanished into thin air. To protect her from self-destruction, he did what he thought was necessary.

Plunging the knife into his own heart, he whispered, "We'll be together beyond this life." He left, not realizing that true love carves countless paths to a single destiny. Separation was his choice.

Ten years later, they met where their story began. The blues of the ocean and sky mirrored their incompleteness without each other. A single glance erased their emptiness, melting the pain away.

Tears streaming, she said, "I thought you'd never come back."

He smiled, replying, "Darling, we were always meant to be."

They embraced for hours in the rain as the moon watched over them and wept with joy. In that moment, she understood sacrifice demands patience, and true love thrives in divine timing.

Not Ordinary

Not ordinary, not fleeting, but rooted deep,
A tribe of strength where secrets sleep.
Criticized, loathed, yet steadfast they stand,
Bound by faith, not by the world's command.

Like unyielding mountains beneath the sky,
They rise when storms and whispers fly.
Their pride is not the haughty kind,
But quiet flames that light the mind.

Warriors born with hearts of steel,
A force the winds of time can feel.
Their love endures, their grudges remain,
Echoes of loyalty, shadows of pain.

They are stars that refuse to fall,
Lighting paths for one and all.
They are winds that shift the earth,
Legends woven from courage and birth.

Can a man, adorned in the finest grace,
Step into battle with a tranquil face?
They fight with honor, a purpose divine,
Their roots entwined in history's spine.

They are walls of strength, foundations of gold,
Guardians of stories the ages have told.
Their eyes, like mirrors, reflect devotion,
A love unbroken, as vast as the ocean.

Unified yet unique, their hearts ignite,
A flame that glows through the darkest night.
Their devotion whispers through the land,
A rhythm only time can understand.

An unwritten song of old,
Whose echoes endure, whose tales are bold.
Not just a tribe but a legacy's song,
A heartbeat eternal, forever strong.

Test Anxiety

So, students! Ready for the test?
The teacher says, like a boss,
An aura of helplessness,
How am I supposed to pass when I didn't even
study?
The clock acting generous, ticking its hands slower
than ever,
Tension grows,
Heart thumps hard in fear,
And chills go down the spine,
I should know this, I should know this,
I have done it so many times,
The question paper tortures as it comes,
Blocking my thinking skills,
Taking a deep breath,
Trying not to break a sweat, I read it consciously,
Carefully reminiscing what I learned,
And then my heart calms down,
Hand starts writing paragraphs,
Satisfied enough when the paper is gone.

The Threshold of Stars

I had never seen him falter,
Yet his gaze lingered, soft and somber.
The melody swelled, a tide of sound,
Laughter and joy danced all around.

But at the threshold, my steps froze.
Time paused; the world composed.
I clung to the hand that once held my fears,
A fortress of strength through all the years.

"You've grown so quickly," he murmured low,
His hands cupped mine, a warm, silent glow.
Within them, perhaps, lay a fragment of magic,
A blessing to mend what felt so tragic.

I blinked back tears, yet the stream broke free,
And in his embrace, I found clarity.
The love I craved wrapped me whole,
Yet restless tides stirred in my soul.

In the hallway, she stood with grace,
A smile etched lightly across her face.
Our eyes met; I ran to her side,
Seeking a haven where love could abide.

I wanted to vanish, to melt away,
To stay in their arms for one more day.
My stars, my guides, my constant light,
What was I without their might?

Stillness filled the air, a poignant haze,
The parting clouded the joyful blaze.
He led me to the waiting car,
Adorned with roses, sunflowers, and the faintest star.

My heart faltered with each hesitant stride,
A battle waged between fear and pride.
The door closed, and as the engine turned,
My fingers sought his touch, unconcerned.

The road unfurled, the world reshaped,
My life transformed, destiny draped.
Beside me sat the man, now bound,
His voice a weight, a solemn sound.

"Do not cry; all is well by His grace."
The words echoed in the silent space.
A gentle solace or a quiet decree?
I could not discern what it meant for me.

The car sped forward, a relentless tide,
Into a future where love would abide.
But in my heart, a fragment remained —
The stars I left, their light unrestrained.

Echoes of the Forgotten Light

The unmade road stretched, a shadow at its side,
Land scattered with life as time seemed to glide.
Through countless jolts, I inhaled the cold air,
Branches cut the sky, trees reaching with care.
Hills stood upright, marching by the moon's
command,
While caterpillars sang in rose bushes, unplanned.

Abandoned homes whispered secrets, sealed tight,
Hiding the traces of forgotten light.
The village hospital, not grand nor adorned,
Filled with pale scents and souls forlorn.
Patients unchecked, their needs untold,
As lizards danced in the lamps, growing bold.

Walls worn by storms, time's cruel embrace,
The air thick with mystery, an unspoken space.
A brilliant doctor with wisdom constrained,
Like a child lost, yet unrestrained.
His eyes, almond-shaped, his nose aquiline,
Resembling an eagle, sharp and divine.

Wrinkles formed as he squinted with care,
Focused and occupied, unaware.
The well-dressed man, whose place was unclear,
Had little but knowledge, sincere.
Medicines lined like books on a shelf,
While hygiene was forgotten, lost to oneself.

Lizards, grand as serpents, crawled in the dark,
As the queue swelled, each patient a mark.
"He's known for his skill," a voice did declare,
"Last night, when my mother needed care,
He rose without hesitation to treat with grace.
A learned man, his wisdom in place."

"He's always there, a heart full of light,"
Said the nurse in white, stained with yellow despite.
Generosity coursed in his every breath,
A man whose kindness defied the depths.

Flies exhaled in a tempestuous swarm,
While footsteps retreated, leaving no form.
I drove back, jolts rattling the way,
Surprised by the silence of a path led astray.
A decade passed, yet the darkness remained,
The engine of my trust by betrayal stained.

Then, an angel's hand lifted me from despair,
A prick revived me from stagnant air.
The light, once blinding, was lost to the night,
A fleeting beacon, now out of sight.

The Moon Between Us

Funny what obsession can do,
A warning to those who love too true.
Love is a game, but trust, the king,
Without it, what does love to bring?

What's love without trust in the heart?
What's trust without love to start?
I can't fix a broken soul,
Just want to drive and lose control.

To vanish in the blackened night,
Absorb the stars, feel their light.
To drink the elixir from above,
And watch my wounds heal with love.

I want to rise, I want to fly,
But the space between us burns, oh my.
Like the moon, I'm always there,
Even when you cannot see or care.

In Your Love

My heart can't stay without yours,
You write my soul in love's pure course.
I long to cry in your pain,
To heal the wounds that leave a stain.

I yearn to hear your voice so near,
To get lost in you without fear.
I want to see you in my dreams,
And feel your breath in silent streams.

I want to be the one you seek,
The only love you ever speak.
I just want to be yours, my dear,
Forever near, forever clear.

Living Inside Him

He must have stayed awake all night,
Perhaps his tears fell out of sight.
They don't fall without a cause or rhyme,
A heart that prays for him lost in time.

My heart has cried, my heart has wept,
In silent love, its promises kept.
I've lost control, my soul now still,
Living inside him, against my will.

Harmony of Love

I think of you all day, all night,
Time itself bears witness to this plight.
What more can I give, what more to do?
I float in your thoughts, so deep, so true.

How do you want me to love you, dear?
In every storm, I'll be near.
Through all seasons, we'll walk as one,
Facing trials until they're gone.

Why test me so? My heart does beat,
For you, my love, in rhythm sweet.
You are my life, my soul's delight,
You are my harmony, my guiding light.

Together Forever

How can I forget our first rain of love?
A gift so pure, sent from above.
I long to fulfill all your dreams,
Without you, my love's not as it seems.

Connect your heart with mine, so true,
Forget the world, just me and you.
Hold my hand, and don't look back,
We're meant to be, no love we lack.

Melody of Fire and Hope

You are the smile upon my lips,
The melody beating within my heart.

A fire ignites the ego, chasing the shine,
Never pausing for a glance behind.

Feet tread upon a blanket of burning coal,
A storm meant to crush like a damaged can.
Yet it ignites dead holes into cracking fireworks,
Turning ruin into bursts of light.

Rainstorms create streams of darkness,
But they dissolve in the dawn of fierce firestorms.
Hardships arrive with unexpected luck,
A bucket of cheers amidst the trials.

Comprehend the faith and tear across the sky,
Like shooting stars that burn and inspire.
Enlighten hope instead of destroying it—
A magical melody in every nook and corner,
Where even devils falter and retreat.

Yet soon, the melody strikes a stone heart,
And infinite numbness takes its place.

Deadly Alive

Love, once a fallen angel,
Turned out to be a devil in disguise.
What seemed like a promise
Unraveled into a cruel game.

The air grew heavy with an impatient, steady aura,
A silent reminder of betrayal,
Lingering like a shadow.

Negativity crept in,
Clouding the mind with its relentless grip.
Memories blurred, and truth
Became a distant echo.

The heart struck with sharp blows,
Felt like a chisel hammering deep into its core.

In the solitude of the room,
Limbs curled tight, head buried low,
Tears flowed endlessly.
The darkness, sweet yet suffocating,
Offered an embrace no light could pierce.

The heart was lost, the mind frozen.
Alive—yet painfully so.
A state of being deadly alive.

The Beauty of Life's Trials

Life holds a quiet beauty when seen simply,
Yet, we often complicate it.
Challenges are fleeting,
But we make them linger,
Turning passing moments into permanent shadows.

Acceptance can be our strength—
Facing trials with quiet resilience,
Trusting that life holds unseen wonders for us all.

Every hardship is a test to overcome,
A step closer to something greater.
Let us not rush to judge others,
For understanding belongs to a place beyond us.

"After every storm, there is calm."
Live not for the approval of others,
But with purpose and hope
For brighter days ahead.

The Ghost of Glory

When the candles flushed, the sins shone bright—
So bright she could no longer bear the glare.
Her retinas swelled, reflecting memories that stung,
While harsh lullabies echoed in her ears.

Disappointment surged, and ghostly tears emerged,
Howling like wolves in the night.
She yearned for the gem—those days of glory—
Lost in the haze of memory, she refused to revisit.

Yet, determination ignited within,
Enlightening her wounded ego.
The demons, once tormenting her soul,
Were exorcised forever.

The Path of

Innocent Destruction

I remember those nights when sleep was a stranger,
When just a few words could light up my world.
A single name became my universe,
Making everything else feel distant and unreal.

Even a disastrous omen—a portent of death—
Seemed sweet in that solemn ambiance.
Deranged, like a stubborn child chasing the
forbidden,
Surrounded by good deeds, yet craving love.

She knew, deep inside, that this love would destroy
her,
But her innocence blinded her heart.
She carved a path for herself, unaware
That it led to ruin.

And so, she surrendered to destruction,
Allowing herself to be undone
In the most intimate and deliberate ways.

The Deception of Innocence

Those soothing vibes when the sun rose,
The mesmerizing beauty of flowers—so distinct.
The happiness felt when birds chirped,
Dew drops so fresh, like crystals.

My sufferings suddenly sought a cure
In that pure, untouched ambience.
My heart slept soundly, like a newborn,
While the cold breeze swept me into an unbelievable
fantasy.

In this world, trees were as large as houses,
Mountains touched the clouds,
And I stood, awestruck by snowfall in summer.

Born between the rivers of danger,
Where love was a deception, trust a mistake,
Truth denied, and fakery believed.

The Ruin of Misconception

Can you love the same person for the second time?
Break a plate and say sorry—will the plate be whole
again?
When your heart falls in love, it shatters into pieces—
Pieces that can never be truly joined.

When you break a heart, it deceives the mind,
And the mind, overwhelmed by deception,
Fills the old scars with a false perception of
happiness.
We yearn for goodness and cross our limits,
Lost in this misconception.

Little do we realize that in our ignorance,
We drown ourselves,
Until we are beautifully ruined.

The Tapestry of Trials

Life is filled with countless ups and downs.
It is a journey, not a ready-made dress.
Every path where we have bled —
Karma leaves its mark, blood red.

It is, in essence, an unseen examination
That many of us fail to truly understand.
Often, we find ourselves drowning
In the never-ending pool of regrets.

Yet, we must rise, like a shooting star,
Draw strength and trust in the process.
We should not be overwhelmed by the haze of
materialism,
But focus on self-improvement,
Patiently working toward becoming
The best version of ourselves.

For hasty actions often lead us astray,
While patience and intention guide us forward.

The Weight of Betrayal

How painful was the trauma—an unbearable ache.
Insomnia settled in. That beautiful mask,
Disguised in innocent spark, crept over her
Like a lion with satin jaws.

Eyes that once gleamed with affection
Now portrayed an unexpected betrayal.
Lips that once spoke words of love
Now poured out unbearable lacerations,
Gradually wearing away the skin.

Limbs numb, acting in parallel to her weakness,
Her soul was sharply torn.
She went against her morals,
Denying the conscience that constantly stabbed her,
Wandering blindly in a world of misconception.

Now she lies in bed,
The terrible devil appears before her eyes—
Memories sinking her into a trance.
Lips force a smile,
And the tears justify the pain of her ego.

Then, the soul rests,
Neglecting the negativities,
While a sense of determination rises above the
bruises.

The Path to Light

Every path we stumble upon may lead us to a new
ray of sunshine.
People come and go, guided by forces beyond our
understanding,
And often, greater plans are unfolding for us—
Something we may not always see.

Don't trust those insidious thoughts.
They often disguise themselves as beauty,
Yet they lead us astray.
Struggling, holding on to the past, or staying in pain
Won't heal the wounds of the heart.
It will only deepen them,
Opening the door for negativity to take hold,
Threatening to overshadow our better selves.

Let the darkness pass,
But don't give it control—
Offer it only a passing glance, not your full embrace.

A Path of Patience

Every step we take, every breath we draw,
We must call upon Him and embrace patience.
His love for us is endless,
And despite our flaws, He grants us all we desire.
So be grateful, and wait for the right time to unfold.

Never let sorrow take hold of what is taken from you;
Something greater awaits in the future.
His doors are always open—
Be patient, be kind.

Live in such a way
That those who don't know Him
Are drawn to His light.

A Freedom Found

How light-burdened she felt when she poured out the
thorns
Once buried deep inside, suffocating her every day.
Life, then, became so organized,
Like vibrant flowers in a vase.
Her wings spread wide,
Ecstatic, like a bird freed from its cage.

She inhaled positivity,
As a tree inhales the air that sustains it.
She was no longer a stationary figure,
Left behind in the whirlwind of life.
For the first time, she truly understood her journey.

Laughter, once silenced,
Now echoed from a heart that had been locked for so
long.
She found a remedy,
A key to her heart's infinite chambers,
And then the key disappeared, never to return.

The fragrance of change filled her world,
Like autumn's touch on leaves,
Her wounds, once caused by darkness,
Now healed by the freedom of expression—
A freedom no one would take from her again.

The Depths of Severance

Within her, she was a thousand others.
Severance so severe, like a drought in a garden.
She could no longer drift between gloom and high
delight.

How satisfying it was to watch those words burn to
ashes,
Into a mystery that seemed infinite.
So organized, like an ant, the game was well played.
The spark diminished into thin air, leaving no trace.

She inhaled loneliness like an alcoholic drinks
alcohol.
Words spread quickly: love is deception.
He got what he wanted and threw her heart
Into the deepest of oceans,
Where she feared being played again,
Afraid of reminiscing about her beautiful scars.

Embers in the Wind

The scrumptious aroma fills the air,
A wave of exodus, both sweet and rare.
Distinct yet comforting, it lingers near,
As we leave behind what we hold dear.

Excitement stirs for the homeland's embrace,
While sorrow follows, a soft, silent trace.
Life is fleeting, like petals in the wind,
A moment's breath and time begins to spin.

Cherish each second, for it's never still,
A fleeting treasure shaped by will.
Like a mother's touch, tender and pure,
Time slips away—yet we endure.

Opportunities, like rubies, glow bright,
We all possess the knowledge to take flight.
But how we use it, and the paths we chart,
Are the bridges we build, or the gaps we impart.

Eternal Bond

He stood in silence, weathered yet resolute,
A flame burning steady against the winds of longing.
Across the divide, another flame flickered brighter,
But his glow, though modest, held a warmth
unmatched.

Dreams whispered to him in the still of night,
Echoing in the depths of his quiet sighs.
"I wish I could give the world," murmured the
shadows of his thoughts,
Yet his heart, steadfast, replied with a gentle hymn of
trust.

His love, a stream pure as sacred waters,
Seeped into cracks that riches could not fill.
As striking as the tang of life's simplest joys,
It wrapped itself around a weary soul like sunlit
tendrils of ivy.

Promises were not spoken but felt in the silence,
Where care outshone the richest gold,
And hope anchored itself like a lighthouse to
wandering ships.
Even the most delicate breeze carried his quiet
strength,
An unseen force brushing past, leaving footprints of
faith.

Paths diverge like rivers to the sea,
Yet every current carries its share of dreams.
Some drift in gilded boats, others swim through tides
of gratitude.
But all seek the same shore—
Where love, unmeasured, eternal, awaits.

Echoes Within

Someone watches, silent and knowing,
as my heart aches to stay near yours.
I feel unseen strings pulling us closer,
A story unfolding beyond our sight.
I weep for your pain, yearning to mend
the invisible scars that linger within.

In quiet moments, I send my pleas—
Let me be written into your world.
Did sleep evade you?
Were your tears unspoken?
Even my lashes glisten not without cause,
Reflecting the weight of your silence.

I long for your voice,
To drift away in the vastness of you.
This heart prays, cries, and loves—only you.
I no longer belong to myself.
I wander somewhere deep in your essence.

Thoughts of you blur time's edges,
And still, I wonder, what more can I give?
I lose myself in the rhythm of your presence,
Yearning to meet the unspoken needs of your soul.
Through every storm, every fleeting season,
I remain steadfast and untested.

You are the pulse within my veins,
A whisper in every quiet breath.
Time bears witness to the distance between us,
As I linger on the edge of your dreams,
Still bound to you in every heartbeat.

Whispers of Longing

Our memories, our fleeting meetings,
How could I forget that rain of love?
You are my heart, my very life,
Won't you come closer, just once?

Let your eyes meet mine,
Let our hearts align.
Don't lower your gaze,
Don't turn away.
Don't forget me, don't move on—
Return the love I've earned, the love I deserve.

I am lost, consumed by you,
longing to wander within your depths,
To uncover the wounds you hide.
Why do you stay so distant?
Why does your silence ache like a storm?

My love remains with you,
But without you, love feels undone.
It's fate—our meeting must complete the circle.
Return the spark that once was mine.

Run through my veins once more,
Lend strength to this weary heart.
Awaken my soul again,
And make me whole,
As only you can.

Whispers of Devotion

I want to share your pain,
To soothe the wounds, you keep within.
Your voice is a calm I yearn for,
A place where my restlessness fades.

My heart has silently wept for you,
loved you without pause,
Lost itself in your essence.
I dream of meeting you in moments unseen,
To be the one who lingers,
quiet but certain,
In every breath you take.

Fated Hearts

Return the love I truly deserve,
This restless heart is lost in your curve.
I yearn to journey deep within,
To find the scars you hide within.

Why do you stray so far from me?
My love is yours; it's meant to be.
Without you, life feels so incomplete,
Our meeting is fated, our hearts must greet.

Bring back my spark, run through my veins,
Strengthen my heart, dissolve the pains.
Reinvigorate my soul, make it whole again,
Let us live beyond this world's disdain.

I'll steal your dreams and make them mine,
Together, we'll live a love divine.
Forget the world, just take my hand,
Don't look back —we're meant to stand.

In Your Essence

You have captured my heart,
For you, I would soar through flames,
For you, I would walk on thorns.
There's something entirely unique about you,
Your eyes speak stories untold,
Your smile is my haven of peace.

You've connected me to your frequency,
You are the constant channel in my life,
The bond between our hearts is unbreakable,
The rhythm your gaze sends through me only
deepens my desire.

You are my favourite melody,
Your love taught me to embrace vulnerability,
It taught me to live with the thrill of the unknown,
Your love has become my essence,
Your scent lingers, touching my soul completely.

The Chains We Breathe

I open my eyes and catch a glimpse of why I breathe,
I feel a stranger pulling at me, trying to tear me
beneath.
The more I try to offer clarity, the more hate I meet,
A thousand dreams remain incomplete in this unfair
deceit.

My soul lies in my palm, and so I give a reason for my
breath,
To be a witness to the mesmerizing beauty is what I
dreamt.
A dream of endless visions drifting through the air,
Competing ruthlessly, chasing fleeting desires in
despair.

I believe in our unbreakable dreams,
I believe in our strength, echoing through lost hopes
and streams.
I see the day when we'll be free to choose our own
path,
When the stranger within will dive into oceans of
freedom at last,
Never longing to return to the suffocating dungeon's
grasp.

To some, we are more dead than alive,
The ones who can't see our blood turning black,
The ones who can't witness our once-glowing skin
now turning pale.
I close my eyes, picturing better days to come,
And when I open them, I catch a glimpse of why we
still breathe.

A Dance in the Fire

She swallowed the fire, knowing it would burn,
She embraced the risk and let herself yearn.
For others, the fire was a game of insane delight,
For her, it was the first sip of an elixir that felt right.

She danced in the flames like never before,
Letting the pain flow in laughter galore.
The cold, buried metal beneath her skin,
Tranquilized her emotions, locked within.

The moon in the dark sky, her deadly foe,
Stars crept closer like demons below.
No longer could she drift in beauty's disguise,
Every nook and corner held memories of his lies.

She couldn't find bliss in his lingering thoughts,
Nor sleep in the warmth of the nights she once
sought.
Her love, deep as the universe's core,
Now left her vulnerable, unable to ignore.

Her heart, a burden she could not bear,
She longed to give it to someone who cared.
She wanted to be loved, but not with such force,
Not without a heart, yet love was her course.

Galactic Enigma

I want to keep you all to myself,
I want to hold you safe in my heart,
Shield you from everything that could hurt you,
And keep your smile never torn apart.

Our enigma is unlike any other,
A blend of water and fire, unspoken,
An impossible puzzle that no one can decipher,
In its mystery, we're both broken.

Your scent is a magnet that pulls me deep,
Into the pool of unconsciousness, where we meet,
Where our shadows intertwine and take flight,
In a world where we soar without a second thought
in sight.

Under the trees, our hands fit perfectly,
The stars unite as they gaze at us,
Like galaxies forming with every touch,
Their lights burn brighter because of us.

Don't leave me now, for once you do,
The galaxies will shatter and fall apart,
Leaving scars of despair and tears of regret,
Breaking everything we built in the heart.

Moonlit Despair

Lost in the hypnosis of the moon,
My body ached,
Yet I searched endlessly for his love.
Every wound bled,
Trying to feel the pain.

The waves were furious,
The moon shining full,
While the sky remained pitch black—
Much like my soul.

Grasp That Light!

How many times must you go through this pain?
I remember the last time—it felt so insane.
Indescribable, yet it left me fulfilled,
A lesson learned, yet my heart stood still.

It's hardest when you need it the most,
Finding peace feels like chasing a ghost.
A fine line exists between care and strain,
Cross it, and you'll only feel the rain.

Take all the time to find who you are,
Without your light, you'll never get far.
In search of love and happiness, we roam,
Yet, forget to cherish the peace of our home.

It's time to realize what you truly seek,
It all starts within; make yourself unique.
Love yourself the way you want to be,
Only then can you set your soul free.

Why is it so hard to love your own mind?
You'll disappoint others—leave them behind.
Do it for you, and you won't go astray,
In the end, your heart will lead the way.

It's always you first, don't second-guess,
You're not selfish—just caring, no less.
We all need love and emotional grace,
If they don't understand, let them leave space.

Unbroken

What do you do when your world is suddenly turned upside down? Do you stand still, watching it unravel, or do you feel a pull urging you to act, to make it right?

What could possibly be missing in this world of beauty and wonder? Have you ever felt that something essential is just... out of reach, lingering in the corners of your soul?

The sun spills its golden light over the earth, pigeons glide gracefully, greeting the day, and little girls swing high, their laughter carried on the breeze. It's all so peaceful, so perfect.

The cool wind whispers, soothing my thoughts, while the birds sing and the leaves dance in harmony with the breeze. It's a moment of calm, a space for reflection. And I find myself drifting into memories of days filled with joy, yet even as I reach for them, the answers evade me.

Everything halts. I try to escape—escape from the abyss that threatens to swallow me—but it pulls me back.

Why? I don't understand.

I seek help, yet still, I'm stuck, trapped in the same cycle.

Do you know what this means?

Does it tell me that only the light within can guide me out of this dark place? That the strength to rise above, to meet the darkness head-on, lies within me? I keep searching for that light, and I hope that one day, we will all find the courage to face the shadows, armed with our own brilliance.

My advice?

No one can define your worth—your priorities, your struggles, your intellect, your journey. It's time to paint over that blank canvas with your truth. It's time to confront your fears, to stand tall for yourself—and only for yourself.

Tea, Sun, and Self

Today, I sat on my balcony with a cup of tea, watching the morning sky as the sun's rays illuminated it, how mothers carried their children to school, and how the autumn leaves danced gracefully in the breeze.

I became immersed in a deep sense of awareness, which made me reflect on how life continues, regardless of what surrounds us. It's strange, isn't it? The thought itself gives me goosebumps—and I'm sure it does the same for you.

How can anything be so unpredictable? Isn't it a bit crazy?

But, without arriving at a conclusion, I realized that when your heart and mind move at the same pace, even the most difficult challenges become attainable. So, believe me when I say that to connect with everything else around you, you first need to connect with yourself.

The Burden of Acceptance

Today, I was taken aback by a sudden thought: Why do we dwell so much on certain things? Are we truly in charge of life, after all?

Is it possible that our fate has already been written, and we're simply too unwilling to accept it? And because of that resistance, we feel hurt, drained, and form negative outlooks? Is this all there really is?

Imagine if we could accept whatever comes our way, surrender it to a higher power, and still work hard for the better. Would that really make a difference? And if things still go downhill, what then? Do we still embrace it? Do we still accept it?

We walk into the fire, letting it burn us with a strange sweetness. But in the end, is this suffering even worth it?

Exodus

I wonder if it's okay to feel this way…
The clock ticks, the wind whirls, and my heart
plummets with every breath I take.

I painted a butterfly today — quite unique, I must
say.
It was vibrant and free, but I wasn't.

Is it possible to be happy without being free?

A wave of thoughts perplexes me…
I hop from one dot to another with no strings
attached.
I keep jumping, but this web consumes me.

The ticking grows louder, and the whirling startles
me, but somehow, I catch my breath.
I run and run as far as I can, with no limits.

A distant rainfall catches my gaze.
How strange it seems in a world like this.
I enter a new era — rainbows, glitter, and giggles.

It makes me wonder:
How far do we need to run before we find ourselves?

Fleeting Light

Life can twist, it can unfold,
With memories of days gone cold.
The sun, the wind, they all seem near,
Yet something's missing; it's unclear.

I flee the abyss, yet I'm still bound,
A light within, where hope is found.
The struggles rise, the darkness calls,
But within me, that light still stands tall.

Rebirth

Today, I say, "It's just you now,"
No more to lose, no more to bow.
The pain, the hurt, it's all behind,
It's time to grow; it's time to find.

The blank canvas, my new start,
I face my fears; I heal my heart.
No one can define my way,
I rise again with each new day.

The Inner Quest

A journal begins, a life to write,
With hopes and dreams that feel so bright.
The world around is wild and free,
Yet I seek freedom inside of me.

The clock ticks on, I stand and stare,
The light I seek is somewhere there.
Through all the chaos, I still believe,
That self-love is what I must achieve.

A Path Unfolding

I'm stuck, I'm lost, I don't quite know,
But through the dark, a light must glow.
A journey long, a path unclear,
But still, I walk without my fear.

The world may change, the days may pass,
But in the end, I'll find my class.
With courage, strong, and hope to show,
The future's bright; it's time to grow.

The Certain Truths

There are situations too complex to grasp,
Certain words that are better left unsaid.
Some feelings are best left to pass,
And some people aren't meant for your thread.

There are places that should stay vacant,
And moments best left untouched.
But some thoughts are meant to be radiant,
And dreams that should never be hushed.

Ambitions that rise and make you roar,
Opportunities you must seize with might.
Paths that must be walked, and more—
Ways that can't be changed by sight.

So, grab your chance with strength anew,
Hold your head high and spread your wings.
Ignore the voices that try to skew—
Criticism is just another's strings.

For advice comes from another's view,
Not your own, so don't be confined.
Walk your own path, and you'll break through,
For only you can define your mind.

Love

All those little things—were they just that?
I try to grasp what love truly means.

Is it the morning breakfasts shared in the light?
Is it the late-night cuddles that feel so, right?
Is it the anger that courses through the veins,
Or the pulsating heart that asks you to refrain?

Is it the language spoken across distant lands,
Or simply the key that, in every moment stands,
Unlocking solutions to questions unknown,
Is love just the thread that weaves us alone?

Monotonous – A Drill

"I hear you," it said,
But I still wasn't sure,
I can't find the words; something feels off,
It just doesn't seem right anymore.

"What to do?" it asked,
My thoughts ambushed me,
I don't know where the answers are,
It just doesn't seem right, you see.

It's as if I forgot how to live,
How to find joy, how to forgive.

Are you sure you're not scared to live fully?
Are you sure you're not scared to feel happy, truly?

Is it okay to feel the urge to act,
To be restless when there's nothing to do, in fact?
Is it wrong to seek solace in silence?

"What to do?" it asked me again,
But this time, my thoughts didn't storm in,
I found the answers, but they still wouldn't come,
And it just doesn't seem right; I'm numb.

The Struggle to Rest

A deep sigh fills my chest—
I feel compelled to share how it feels…

Not quite familiar, yet calm—
Not the serenity that comes naturally,
But something much more powerful,
A stillness that commands attention.

"Darling, it's time to rest," it says,
Quite startling indeed.
But see, the thing is—I don't rest;
I keep racing until I crash.

"Rest!" it whispers,
This time, more bossily… but—

It feels better? It feels calm? It feels fulfilling?

Quite the perplexing scenario, you see.
Do I keep racing?
Do I outrun my own heart?
Do I complete the challenges,
Or do I submit, or do I accept?

Oh, dear! A shiver runs through me,
I feel it slowly letting go,
Filling me with excitement—
I can't help but wonder,
Is this what "accepting it" means?

Let Them Be

Doesn't everyone have the right to their own opinion?
To act independently and uphold their own morality?
Why must things always be made so complicated?

Give people the freedom to express themselves
Without needing to justify their actions.
Allow them to be understood,
Without the weight of judgment.
Just let them be themselves.

A thought crossed my mind today,
It stirred my curiosity deeply.
I was overwhelmed by the silence.

Is it not okay for someone to have their own opinion?
To do things their own way and still be right?
Why must everything be made so difficult,
So hard to understand?

Allow people to express themselves
Without having to explain.
Allow them to be understood
Without judgment.
Let them simply be who they are.

Break Free

Be the one you want to share it all,
For no one will truly heed your call.

Talk of communication, words that fade,
When no one's willing to learn, to trade.

Expectations based on what they do,
But leave that bubble—it's not for you.

The world can't see what's deep inside,
So, break free, let your true self reside.

Unleash

Today, once again, I vanish in thin air,
Carrying the burden of a battle so unfair.

Imagine a world where you can do as you please,
Without worrying, living in perfect ease.
I yearn for that world where freedom reigns,
And worries vanish, swept by the winds and rains.

I want to feel the fresh breeze in every land,
To swim across oceans, feeling the sand.
I want to tell you it's okay to make mistakes,
For it's your journey, and it's what it takes.
I want to remind you there's no reason to fear,
That courage lies within, crystal clear.

A dream it is, to turn my "I want tos" to "I did,"
To let go of worries, free from the grid.
To release my soul from this endless strain,
And let my spirit soar, free from the chain.

I believe very few of us have this gift of detachment,
Or is it all just a façade, a mere act, a fraction?
How can I enjoy the moment without the past or
future in sight?
How can I live carefree, with nothing to fight?
How can I free myself from myself?
How can I trust the journey when the path is still
unclear?

Extended Reality

I wander, unsure of what's going on,
Life's not as thoughtless as it seems; is it gone?

I sense fear lurking in these blurred lines,
Once so clear, now tangled in signs.

How can one lose faith in themselves, so unsure?
Living life as if there's nothing to endure.

Something inside me longs for change,
A kind that no one can create or arrange.

Dear, something inside you begs to stop trying,
While something within me shouts to keep defying.

This era of extended reality hides false altruism,
This era of extended reality masks disguised
terrorism.

So, I give up—
I give up on everything, but...

I cling to you,
Hoping I'll find myself again with you.

But hope is all we have, isn't it?

Thus, a simple question arises—what am I truly
thriving for?

The Beauty of Existence

Today, I travelled once again,
A feeling deep, I can't explain.
A quiet stillness, soft and near,
As if a memory reappeared.

I once believed that time would heal,
That feelings fade, and wounds would seal.
But now I know it's not the case—
Feelings hide, then show their face.

They don't fade away, they're here to stay,
They shape our path; they light our way.
Each one a guide, a lesson learned,
A piece of us, forever earned.

And life, oh life, what can I say?
It doesn't just move on its way.
It's kind to me, it lets me grow,
It teaches more than I could know.

I cherish every laugh and tear,
The memories that draw me near.
The moments, both of joy and pain,
That wash me clean like summer rain.

I've learned to love this journey wide,
To feel, to learn, to not divide.
To see the beauty in each breath,
In life's own dance, beyond our death.

So now I fall in love with all—
With dreams, with love, with fate's soft call.
With every moment, pure and bright,
In the beauty of mere life's light.

A Moment Captured

A ray of light, so pure, so bright,
A thought of peace in the still of the night,
A moment captured in fleeting time,
A memory carved in rhythm and rhyme.

What colors can your heart reveal?
Do they reflect what your eyes feel?
Do they echo what your soul yearns for,
A silent call, forever more?

Yearning for Happiness

It is now, I finally see,
That emptiness is yearning to be free.
A cry for joy, for self to find,
For the caterpillar to leave behind.

From misery's grip, it seeks release,
To transform, to find its peace.
A soul reborn, so pure, so bright,
Emerging from the darkest night.

A Long Silence

With all the growing atrocities and violence,
I decide to break my silence.

It's a frustrating situation, & terribly painful,
The fact that I cannot do anything is so disdainful.

I no more find peace in nature,
It's all just filled with war wagers.

"I will tell Him about you when I go there," said one;
"Those animals, like human, deserve to die", said
another, their hearts undone.

Labelling and being labelled is a vicious violation,
One soul passing after another is also a horrendous
infliction.

My aching heart seeks a path to closure;
Their aching heart yearns for a peaceful composure.

A silence that echoes louder than ever before;
Shattering screams across the globe— a call for peace
that we cannot ignore.

A shadow lurks among them to free the pain,
Cruel deaths & inhumane detainment, a world gone
insane.

Inhabiting not only childhood memories but hard-
earned labor,
Yet painting them as violent & destructive neighbors.

An empty bosom stained with the blood of innocent,
Tears flowing down like a never-ending flood of
discontent.

Little fellows filled with fear, tension, & worry,
In an age where you & I were carefree & merry.

The blood-red sky isn't just what we see,
Collapsed buildings and bodies aren't a painful
reality.

Resilient mothers, keeping their loved ones warm;
Compassionate fathers, finding moments of
playfulness in the storm.

A story of freedom buried for generations,
A tale of survival, unspoken for generations.

A persistent yearning for peace, it will never cease,
A tormented endurance, seeking a release.

The struggles, the pain, and the cries you bear are all
heard,
The animosity, the hatred, and the envy towards you
are all observed.

Let compassion be the bridge for this story etched in
history's tapestry,
Generosity and unity forming a future of lasting
prosperity?

In this land of strength, may justice forever reign,
Where freedom thrives, and love erases pain.

A land where broken dreams will once again take
flight,
Unconquerable against the devil's wicked plight.

A Piece of Me

Every time I travel, anxiety takes hold,
As if a piece of my soul is left untold.

Silence rings deep within my chest,
I struggle to find the words to express.

It feels like we leave parts of ourselves behind,
Haven't you wondered how others perceive your
mind?

Thinking about this, I realize with clarity,
Personalities have power; they shape reality.

If they hold influence, they can bring change,
But who, I wonder, is truly making a difference in this
range?

Look deep within, and ask yourself true,
Are you the person you truly want to be, too?

If not, then now is the time, dear,
Change starts within, so let go of your fear.

Seize the moment, embrace what's in sight,
And craft the best version of yourself; take flight.

A Peaceful Moment

A peaceful moment, I suppose it was,
A clear blue sky, calm clouds, gentle breezes, and
falling leaves.

It took a while for me to hear your voice,
And then I knew love exists only in the heart,
nowhere else, by choice.

So, if ever you seek me, near or far,
Close your eyes, feel the breeze, and I'll be where you
are.

Talking softly, whispering true,
In every breeze, my love will reach you.

Second Chance

I often wonder,
What would it be like if fate turned back the page?

When I see you,
Would I freeze, entranced by your face?
Could I welcome you, or would my heart race?

My hands shake as I write,
The thought of your touch — soft, familiar, bright.
Your smile — gentle, enchanting, and true,
Your eyes — like gems that gleam through the blue.

When I see you,
Would my tears fall like rain?
Could I believe you're here again?

When I see you,
Would I awake from this dream so long?
Could I finally hold you where I belong?
Could I speak of the ache, the sorrow untold,
And find in your arms the warmth I once knew?

Would I finally ask the winds to turn,
To carry us back, to let us return?
Would we build new paths and fill the old seams,
With moments forgotten and unspoken dreams?

Countless thoughts,
Countless tears,
No answers come,
No comfort clears.

I wait in silence,
For the day to show its hand,
When the question unfolds:
Must we let go when we don't understand?

The Language of Nature

"Oh! What does nature tell you?" he asked.
"It doesn't really talk to me," I said.
"Then why are you so obsessed with it?" he
questioned.

I paused, thinking.
"It's because nature is where I never doubt that
beauty exists, even in the simplest of creations.
And if I ever feel like giving up, nature is the only
place where I can find perseverance, happiness,
and the strength to keep going."

The Great Escape

When I was young, I dreamed of flight,
Soaring high, among stars, beyond clouds and night.
I thought it a gathering of souls long gone,
A reunion of light where I'd always belong.

But it didn't last, and soon I soared higher,
The sky turned dark—both threatening and dire.
Lost in shadows, yet strangely at peace,
The lights below flickered like fireflies released.

Then came a whisper, soft as a sigh,
One single word: "Life," drifting from the sky.
And with it, a weight came crashing down—
Life is a fleeting dream, swift as it flows,
From one milestone to another, as the river grows.

It never halts, never slows its pace,
Forever in motion, with time in its race.
This truth swept me from the colors below,
Leaving me with one thought I now know:

Keep moving forward, no matter the strain,
For one day, you'll escape—free from life's chain.
And when that moment comes, embrace it with grace,
Hold it, cherish it, never let it waste.

Unwavering Love

There are times when things feel light,
Lighter than they should, shining bright.
There are times when you smile,
More than usual, for a little while.

There are times when all feels natural,
More than it should, almost magical.
I used to wonder what moments are worth,
What makes a memory, and what gives it birth?

Is it a kiss beneath the moon's soft light,
On a quiet evening, holding you tight?
Or a whispered word on a summer breeze,
As we walk together, hearts at ease?

But as I reflect, there's one thing I see,
The most cherished moment is someone with me.
Someone who annoys, yet you don't want them to
leave,
Someone who comes back after a fight to relieve.

Someone who will never give up, no matter the test,
A soul that stays, offering love at its best.
It's rare to find such a love, so true,
But with that soul, you'll always get through.

This is the love I was longing to find,
The love that stays, with no reason to bind.
The love that brings smiles, with just their embrace,
The love that remains, no matter the space.

The love that sticks forever by your side,
A love that can never be replaced never denied.
Would these moments be the ones I'd treasure,
With you beside me, a love beyond measure?

Winter's Bloom

Do you ever think of a winter's bloom?
I mean—summer's bloom, autumn's bloom, spring's
bloom, but winter's bloom?

I don't know where to start with my winter bloom…

It's both quiet and noisy—like a tree playing a flute in
the darkest of its days.
It's both surprising and daunting—like a newborn
struggling to take its first breath.
It's both irritating and painful—like a secret lover
trying to control her emotions.

Letting silence fill me, I walk briskly, searching for the
beat of my heart.
I find myself standing in a room of darkness, reaching
out for the one light.

My winter bloom revolves around me as the earth
turns toward the sun.
My winter bloom is that woodwind seeking peace in
the harshest of hours.

How often do you experience this winter's bloom?

Misty Morning

One misty morning, I woke up next to you,
You slept soundly, like a dream, so true.
Your face gleamed softly in the sunlight's rays,
I wished this moment would forever stay.

One misty morning, I woke up next to you,
Our hearts in sync, as if we always knew.
How I traced the outline of your lips on mine,
Imagining our bond, ever strong, divine.

Peaceful it was, always by your side,
My heart was full of love I couldn't hide.
I didn't want to let you slip away,
But our shadows no longer stayed as one that day.

Then, one misty morning, I dreamt of us,
Laughing, playing, in our love, so just.
A blooming love, fresh and bright,
Always together, holding on tight.

But this misty morning, you were not there,
A silent cry was all I could share.
I reached for you, but you were gone,
This misty morning, I couldn't carry on.

Worth of a Lifetime

A lifetime's worth of advice: no one will ever be like you.

"All you have to do is live for yourself." That's what people say, right? "If someone wants to be there for you, they will be there for you no matter what."

I've spent my entire life looking for someone who can handle me at my worst. Would I do the same if it were up to me?

Another question: Why am I unable to be that person for myself?

Life is a series of unanticipated and unexplained events, but believe me when I say that the best thing it does is make you know who you truly are!

Stop hiding behind your own self-created veil, confront the reality, face yourself, and embrace it. This will allow you to become that person for yourself.

On Occasions

In fleeting whispers, thoughts drift by,
Caught in a dance beneath the sky.
They speak in hues, rich and profound,
Yet their true meaning leaves me unbound.

I ponder their wishes; what do they seek?
In the chaos of silence, I find myself weak.
Do you find it hard to decode your own mind?
In the maze of your musings, clarity's hard to find.

Let's join hands and cast off the weight,
Release the "should" and embrace our fate.
As we wander, feast, and venture afar,
Let's savour the moments, for life's a bright star.

To be here, to be now, is our sweet refrain,
In the tapestry of living, joy we'll attain.
So let's cherish the day, let worries take flight,
In this present, our hearts shine bright.

Through the Inferno

I often sit and ponder perplexing thoughts,
Thoughts so overwhelming they cause my mind to
lose its grasp.

Do I notice things I once missed, or has disorientation
claimed me?

Sometimes, it takes time to clear my vision —
Until the inferno strikes,
And I see eerie shadows smiling in the fog,
Sinister, as if possessed by something darker.

The crystals forged from the wounds of my past
Are inescapable, yet they show me a beautiful path to
change.
A lesson learned:
It's not as pleasurable as a fleeting sin,
But the humility that grows within me
Urges me to step into a world
Where kind words replace harsh whispers,
And rumors fade into silence.

The beam of light piercing my eyes
Is often ignored,
Comforting myself with the belief that another chance
will come.

I strengthen my resolve,
Not by worrying about the voices of doubt,
But by striving to be good,
Not in the eyes of a lost world,
But in the presence of a quiet power—
An unseen force offering a path through the darkness,
A space where brokenness can be healed,
And redemption, though distant, lingers in the air.

The Open Book

Let your soul be an open book and your heart the key
to your perception.
Let your eyes be the windows to your hidden
happiness.
Hold the sleeve, not the hand.

Sometimes, you have no control over the bad
memories.
Cry your heart out — that's where you learn to deal
with them.
Don't let them alter the path of your success.

The Moment Within

I am always nervous, uptight when I travel,
As if a piece of my soul has vanished.
With silence ringing inside my chest,
I can't seem to find a word to express.

Everywhere we go, we leave a bit behind,
A mark of ourselves, unspoken, undefined.
Have you ever looked through another's eyes?
To see yourself from someone else's skies?

Personalities leave their traces, don't you think?
They make an impact; they help us rethink.
We're part of this change, though it's hard to see,
But who is truly shaping what's meant to be?

Look deep within, and ask yourself true:
Is this who you want to be, or is there more to you?
If you haven't yet, now is your moment, dear,
Seize it, and let your best self appear.

Change begins with you; don't wait for the call,
Grab the chance to rise, to become it all.

The Pull of the Void

What do you do when life's turned upside down?
Do you stand still, let it spiral further down,
Or do you feel the urge, the pull to act,
To shift the tides, to take your life back?

What could be missing in this perfect world?
Have you ever felt a void unfurled?
The sun kisses the earth, warm and bright,
Pigeons swoop by, and girls read in delight.

The cool breeze whispers, leaves softly rustle,
An idyllic scene, my heart starts to hustle.
But still, something nags, something feels wrong,
As I search for answers where I don't belong.

A trip down memory lane, I take,
Hoping for clarity, but nothing comes awake.
I try to flee from the abyss, from the dark,
But something pulls me back with an unseen mark.

Why? I don't understand, no words to say,
I rush for help, but I'm stuck in dismay.
Does it mean the light within is the only way?
The only force that can save you today?

I keep searching, hoping for a spark,
For one day, we'll conquer the dark.
Face it with courage, with a spirit that's bright,
And you'll discover how to find your light.

The Struggle Within

The term "struggle" isn't easy, is it?
What's the first thought that you admit,
When you learn that someone's in pain,
Suffering, failing, feeling strained?

But is it truly a struggle that holds one back,
That keeps them from getting on track?
Perhaps you think, "Yes, no, maybe so,"
But the answer's not simple; this much we know.

What if it's self-doubt or lack of drive,
A careless mind that can't survive?
Would you call that a struggle, too,
If the strength within you starts to slip through?

Would you just give up and take a fall,
Refrain from trying, not trying at all?
Would you keep doing what you despise,
Just because it feels hard to cut ties?

Would you hurt yourself, lose your esteem,
Letting your willpower shatter the dream?
Or would you look for a brighter side,
Focus on good, and let hope be your guide?

Would you sink into regret and sorrow,
Wishing for a better tomorrow?
Would you keep leading a life full of pain,
A cycle of flaws, failure, and strain?

The choice is yours; it's yours to make,
To rise above or let it break.
If you don't leave what hurts behind,
You'll never find peace or peace of mind.

Take that step, make the change today,
And you'll love the choice you made, I say.

Detachment

A world — spinning like a rollercoaster, I see,
But I am stuck in a place, you, see?
I don't know if it's me who's frozen or whether it's
time.
I see the lights on the road move faster than mine.

Is it true that light travels faster than anything?
Then why is it still too slow for me?
Every little, tiniest detail of life is being felt by me—
It's just too much for my dear soul, you, see?

I can't figure out whether it's day or night.
Someone pinch me—I might be daydreaming, please.
How the day goes on doesn't make sense anymore,
Such a monotonous thing that keeps recurring, you
see?

I don't remember when, how, or why,
But I don't have dementia, I see.
I never knew that the mere feeling of wouldn't be
enough.
I never knew detachment creeps in when you least
expect it, you see.

It's quite complicated, I must tell you,
Too much is going on with one person, I warn you.
Not just freedom, peace, or love is at stake,
But were they ever truly there, you see?

All I hear are muff_ed sounds, and all I see are
question marks,
A purposeful state caught in a trance, I guess.
It's an empty space to live in for the rest of time,
But can I find the light, you see?

A sense of derangement has been lingering far too
long,
That feeling of being naked, without the actuality of
it.
How do you spend your day? I think.
How are you oriented in time, space, and
consciousness?

Is it possible to live in multiple places at once,
you see?
To feel multiple emotions at once, you see?
Hold onto a certain thread that might take you
somewhere, I advise.
Otherwise, you'll stay in this unpleasant seat,
Daydreaming about your next, I tell you.

All the love in the world, yet I think I am unworthy of
it, you, see?
Nature itself speaks a thousand words,
But I hear none, you, see?

Silent Shores

Is it true that light travels faster than just about
anything?
Then why does it seem so slow to reach me?
Every tiny detail of life feels magnified —
Too much for my dear soul, too vast, you see.

Like a traveller burdened with treasures not their
own,
Crossing distant shores, far from home.
The weight of dreams that are not their own dreams,
Heavy as silence, loud as unseen screams.

What if they could lay it all down —
The expectations, the crowns, the frowns?
What if they could, for just one breath,
Unravel the knots, escape the depth?

The world moves fast, yet I stand still,
A vessel too full, too fragile to fill.
Is it too much to ask for some reprieve —
A moment of quiet, a space to breathe?

The Space Between Us

I trace the contours of your smile,
In memories that stretch for miles.
The spaces between us are wide and vast,
Yet my thoughts of you still hold fast.

I remember how your laughter would fill the air,
Like a breeze, gentle, without a care.
But now, it's silence that lingers in place,
A stillness that echoes your empty space.

The world moves on, but I stand still,
A heart caught between love and will.
I wonder, do you ever pause,
To feel the weight of the unspoken cause?

There's beauty in the space that lies between,
In the moments that remain unseen.
But sometimes, I wish that time would bend,
And we could return to the places we've been.

In the quiet, I hold on to the past,
To the love we had, to the moments that last.
And though the distance may stretch and grow,
I carry you with me wherever I go.

The Dance of Time

We dance through time with steps unknown,
Wandering through seasons, hearts full of hope,
Each moment, a beat, a rhythm we share,
In the quiet spaces, we find love's air.

The past tugs gently at our sleeves,
A whisper of memories that never leave.
But the present pulls us forward, unseen,
To new horizons, where dreams are green.

Yet time, like sand, slips through our hands,
A fleeting moment, like distant lands.
But even when it seems too fast to hold,
Love remains constant, tender, and bold.

So let us dance, not fearing the end,
For every step taken, we transcend.
The dance of time, the song we sing,
Is a melody that lives within.

Beneath the Willow

Beneath the willow, where shadows fall,
I sit in silence, feeling it all.
The breeze that whispers through the leaves,
A secret shared, a soul that grieves.

The earth beneath me is soft and kind,
A place where my thoughts can unwind.
And though the world spins fast around,
Here, in the stillness, peace is found.

The willow bends yet does not break,
A symbol of strength in what we take.
For life is a dance of joy and pain,
But beneath the willow, I remain.

The Language of Stars

We look to the stars, so far away,
Yet, in their light, we find our way.
They speak in silence, a language so pure,
A story of love that will endure.

Each star a memory, a wish, a dream,
A symbol of the things we cannot seem.
Yet, in the vastness, we feel so small,
But we are part of it, after all.

The stars don't ask for anything,
They simply shine in their own spring.
A reminder that in the dark of night,
We can still find beauty, still find light.

Echoes of the Heart

There's a whisper in the wind, a call so deep,
It stirs the soul from its quiet sleep.
It's the echo of the heart that longs to be free,
But is tethered by the past it cannot see.

In every beat, in every breath,
There's a rhythm that overcomes death.
The past may linger, the future unknown,
But in this moment, we're not alone.

The heart speaks in echoes, soft but strong,
Telling us where we truly belong.
And though the world may pull us apart,
The echo of love remains in the heart.

Of Rivers and Roads

I've walked many roads, crossed many streams,
Chasing the echoes of forgotten dreams.
The rivers rush, the roads unwind,
Each step I take, I leave behind.

But the road ahead calls me still,
A winding path, a climb, a hill.
The river may change, but it always flows,
A constant companion wherever it goes.

Life is like a river, swift and true,
The roads we travel, old and new.
But no matter where we may stray,
The river and the road will guide our way.

The Garden of Words

Words are seeds that we plant in the soil,
Nurtured by silence, watered by toil.
Some grow tall, reaching the sky,
While others remain low, and yet still try.

Each word has a story, a life of its own,
A reflection of thoughts we've never fully known.
They bloom, and they fade, like flowers in spring,
Yet, in their passing, they always bring.

The garden of words is vast and deep,
A place where secrets and dreams can sleep.
So let us plant them with care and grace,
And watch them grow in time and space.

The Mirror of the Soul

We look in the mirror, searching for truth,
A reflection of the child, the lover, the youth.
But what do we find beneath the glass,
A soul worn by time yet steadfast.

The eyes that once sparkled with dreams untold,
Now reflect the stories, the scars, the gold.
We are more than what the surface shows,
A deep current where the real light flows.

In the mirror of the soul, we see it all,
The strength, the weakness, the rise, the fall.
Yet, in its depths, we learn to grow,
And understand what it means to truly know.

The Call of the Sea

The sea calls to me, a distant sound,
A voice that echoes, soft, profound.
It whispers secrets, old and true,
Of places hidden, skies so blue.

I long to walk its sandy shore,
To hear the waves and nothing more.
The sea holds stories in its tides,
Of journeys taken, of souls that hide.

But though the sea is far away,
Its call remains with me each day.
For in its depths, I know I'll find
A peace that heals my restless mind.

The Seasons of Us

We met in the spring when flowers bloomed,
A time for new beginnings, hearts consumed.
The air was warm, the sky so clear,
We thought that forever was drawing near.

But life, like the seasons, changes fast,
And summer faded, too soon to last.
Autumn brought its colors bright,
But with it came the quiet night.

Now winter's here, cold and still,
And I stand alone on this frozen hill.
But even as the seasons turn,
I carry you with me, a steady burn.

Through the Storm

I've walked through storms, both fierce and wild,
A heart once broken, now reconciled.
The winds may howl, the rain may fall,
But I stand tall above it all.

Each storm teaches a lesson clear,
That strength is found when we face our fear.
The clouds may gather, the sky may roar,
But after the storm, we are restored.

Through every tempest, we find our way,
And with each dawn, there's a brighter day.
For the storm may pass, but we remain,
Stronger for having weathered the pain.

Footprints in the Sand

The shore remembers where we've been,
Each step, each laugh, each fleeting grin.
The tide may come, the waves erase,
But the journey lives in this sacred space.

Footprints fade as moments do,
Yet the path remains steady and true.
For every step, a story untold,
Etched in the sand, forever bold.

And though the sea may take its claim,
The memories linger, just the same.
For footprints in the sand may go,
But in our hearts, they always glow.

The Song of the Forest

The forest sings a quiet tune,
Under the watchful eye of the moon.
The rustling leaves, the whispering breeze,
A symphony among the trees.

Each branch sways in gentle time,
A melody without reason or rhyme.
Yet, in its chaos, there's peace,
A rhythm that brings the heart release.

The song of the forest is old and wise,
A truth reflected in the skies.
And as I walk beneath its shade,
I hear the music nature made.

A House of Memories

This house is more than walls and stone,
It's the echoes of lives it's known.
Laughter rings in every hall,
Whispers linger, soft and small.

The creak of stairs, the swing of doors,
Are chapters in its endless lore.
Each crack and corner holds a past,
A memory made to always last.

And though the years may take their toll,
This house will always hold its soul.
For in its rooms, love still resides,
A shelter where the heart abides.

A Candle's Plea

I burn for you; I light your way,
Yet I shrink with each passing day.
You praise my warmth, my golden glow,
But I wonder, do you truly know?

The price I pay, the wax I shed,
A silent toll for the path you tread.
Still, I'll burn until I'm gone,
For in your light, I still belong.

Midnight Conversations

Tell me, what keeps you awake at night?
Is it the echoes of words left unsaid?
The weight of dreams still out of reach?
Or the way silence feels heavier
When the world is asleep?
We sit here, two wanderers of thought,
Trading secrets with no promises of answers.
The moon listens, and the stars pretend not to.
In the dark, we are more ourselves,
Unfolding like letters never sent.

The Weight of Rain

The rain falls heavy on my skin,
Each drop a story; each drop a sin.
It whispers tales of broken skies,
Of long-lost lovers, unheard cries.

Puddles form where dreams once grew,
Reflecting worlds I never knew.
The rain, relentless, won't refrain,
It drowns my sorrows, heals my pain.

And when it ends, the world feels new,
Cleansed by the tears of skies so blue.
For even rain, in all its might,
Carries hope in its gentle light.

A Banter with Time

"Why do you rush?" I ask the clock.
"I move with purpose, tick by tock."
"But don't you tire of endless race?"
"It's not the journey—it's the pace."

I laugh, "And what of those who lag?"
"They learn that moments never drag.
Life's best lived with no rewind,
So don't waste time—you'll never find."

And with that note, the clock stood still,
A cheeky pause, a fleeting thrill.

Letters I'll Never Send

I've written to you in my mind,
hundreds of times,
But the words refuse to behave.
They scatter like frightened birds
When I reach for them,
leaving behind half-formed thoughts
And echoes of something I meant to say.
Maybe it's better this way.
Some words are too fragile to speak,
Too raw to survive the weight of being heard.
So, I fold them away in the quiet corners of my heart,
And hope you hear them in the silence between us.

Shadows of the Sun

They say shadows follow the sun,
Chasing a race, they've never won.
Yet in their darkness, truths reside,
A world unseen, where fears collide.

The sun may shine, but shadows stay,
A silent witness to life's ballet.
For without them, we'd never see,
The depth of light's complexity.

Wanderlust

The horizon calls, a siren's song,
To places vast, where I belong.
Mountains rise, and rivers weave,
Stories written by those who leave.

The wind carries whispers of lands unknown,
Of ancient ruins, of seeds long sown.
Wanderlust stirs my restless heart,
Each journey's end, another start.

So, I'll follow the path, wherever it bends,
For the road is a lover who never ends.

Banter with the Moon

"Oh, moon, why do you stare so bright?"
"I only borrow the sun's old light."
"But why so pale, so cold, so near?"
"To reflect what humans fear."

"And what is that?" I dared to ask.
"The truth you hide behind your mask.
Yet still, I shine for all to see,
A mirror for your mystery."

A Pause in the Chaos

In the middle of the bustling street,
I found a moment that felt like home.

A stranger smiled—not out of duty,
But as if they saw the storm I carried
And wanted to calm it.

It wasn't much,
But it was everything.

The Art of Falling Apart

To fall apart is an art, they say,
A gentle unweaving of yesterday.
To let the pieces tumble down,
And sit with silence, wear the crown.

But no one tells you how to begin,
Or what it means to break within.
They simply watch, they stand, they stare,
At the masterpiece of your despair.

Yet in the ruin, seeds are sown,
A garden grows where grief has grown.
And what was lost becomes the start,
Of the sacred art of mending the heart.

A Rainy Night

The rain didn't care that the world was asleep.
It tapped on windows, dripped from rooftops,
  And filled the streets with its symphony.

I stood in the doorway,
Watching as the puddles grew,
Wondering if the rain ever stopped to rest— or if it
  simply poured,
As if it didn't know how to do anything else.

And in that moment,
I understood it.

The Sonnet of Unspoken Words

There lies a world where silence rules the tongue,
Where hearts converse in glances, not in sound.
Each gaze a poem, fragile yet unsung,
Each breath a bridge, invisible, profound.

What truths reside in pauses, in the space,
Between the lines, we never dared to write?
What tender secrets linger, leave no trace,
Yet, shape our souls beneath the quiet night?

Oh, love, how eloquent the unvoiced plea,
How loud the ache when words remain untold!
And though I long for speech to set us free,
The silence speaks of truths rarer than gold.

So let us dwell where quiet hearts align,
For unspoken love is still divine.

The Nomad's Farewell

He wandered through the fields of gold,
Through forests deep and skies so cold.
A restless heart, a weary soul,
Forever seeking, never whole.

He left behind the ones he loved,
The shores where youth once brightly roved.
Each step he took, a bond untied,
Yet freedom called, and so he tried.

The road is kind, the road is cruel,
It teaches more than any school.
For every ending, there's a start,
And every journey breaks a heart.

Ode to the Ocean

Oh, mighty ocean, vast and deep,
In your embrace, the secrets sleep.
You cradle ships, you carry dreams,
You hold the moon's eternal beams.

Your waves, they dance, they crash, they sing,
A hymn to life, an offering.
And though you rage, and though you roar,
You're home to life forevermore.

Teach us your patience, boundless, wide,
Your strength that storms cannot divide.
For in your depths, the truth resides,
That life, like you, forever tides.

The Villanelle

of a Love Untamed

I held your hand but could not make you stay,
The wild in you was brighter than the sun.
Some loves are not for taming, so they say.

Your laughter danced like waves on summer's bay,
A fleeting gift, a race already run.
I held your hand but could not make you stay.

I tried to weave the words that might delay
The call of winds, the cry to be undone.
Some loves are not for taming, so they say.

You loved the road, the places far away,
Your heart a map, your soul a loaded gun.
I held your hand but could not make you stay.

And though you're gone, my memories betray—
I'd choose it all, though pain has just begun.
Some loves are not for taming, so they say.

I held your hand but could not make you stay.

The Coffee Shop

The coffee shop smells like regret and new
beginnings.
You sit there, scrolling through memories
You swore you wouldn't revisit.
The barista hums a song no one recognizes,
But it matches the mood—
Bittersweet, like over-brewed tea.
I catch your eye for a moment,
And it feels like the universe just blinked.
What were you looking for in that glance?
A connection?
A distraction?
The answer, I think, is yes.

Soliloquy to the Stars

Do you ever get tired,
Hanging there in an endless sky,
Watching worlds collide,
And lovers break apart?

Do you laugh at our tiny wars,
Our desperate dreams,
Our fleeting joys?

Or do you envy us,
With our fragile lives
That burn so bright
Before they fade?

The Abandoned Town

There is a stillness here,
Not the kind that soothes,
But the kind that lingers—
A ghost of what was.

The paint on the walls peels,
Like memories trying to escape.
Windows gape, hollow-eyed,
Staring at the nothing that grew
Where life once thrived.

But listen closely,
And you can almost hear
The echo of children's laughter,
The creak of rocking chairs,
And a town that once
Breathed with purpose.

A Love Ballad in Passing

I met you where the rivers meet the sea,
A fleeting spark, a whispered melody.
The tides have pulled you far away from me,
But still, I keep the song you gave to me.

Your voice, it lingers in the morning dew,
Your laughter's warmth in every golden hue.
Though time may steal the moments that we knew,
It cannot touch the love I hold for you.

A Villanelle

for the Wandering Soul

The road is long; the stars are few,
A traveler seeks what cannot be,
The world is vast, yet never new.

The heart's a compass, spinning through,
Its needle points to mystery,
The road is long; the stars are few.

Each step brings loss, each loss renews,
A map drawn in epiphany,
The world is vast, yet never new.

And when the journey's done, we rue
The places we forgot to see.
The road is long; the stars are few,
The world is vast, yet never new.

City Nights

Neon spills across the pavement,
A cascade of artificial stars.
The hum of life—engines, laughter, sirens—
Wraps around the night like a second skin.

The city doesn't sleep.
It dreams in bursts of light,
In whispers from shadowed alleys,
And the endless shuffle of footsteps
That write stories on concrete pages.

And here I am,
Just another character
In this pulsing, breathing
Urban symphony.

A Sonnet for the Wind

You rush through fields, a restless, wild caress,
A fleeting kiss that leaves the earth in sway.
You bear no weight, yet carry such largesse —
The scent of rain, the whispers of the day.

You've seen the peaks, the deserts, and the seas,
Yet, never linger, never call one home.
You play with leaves, or topple mighty trees,
A constant wanderer, destined to roam.

And though you're fierce, you cradle me tonight,
Your song a lullaby, your breath my guide.
Oh, wind, you teach the spirit to take flight,
To dance with life, unbound and open-eyed.

To the Late-Night Thinker

Hey, you with the midnight coffee cup,
Scrolling through thoughts, you can't quite sum up.
What's keeping you up—existential dread,
Or just that meme you saw before bed?

You tell yourself, "Just five minutes more,"
But it's 3 a.m., and you're pacing the floor.
Are you solving life's biggest mystery,
Or rethinking your sixth-grade history?

Either way, friend, here's my advice:
Close your eyes, as sleep feels nice.

A Quiet Walk in the Forest

The trees don't ask your name,
Don't care where you've been.
They simply stand,
Silent sentinels of time.

The path beneath your feet
Cradles your weight
Like a mother holding her child.

And in this moment,
You are not your fears,
Not your past.

You are just a soul,
Walking through eternity,
One step at a time.

The Traveler's Tale

Across the seas and winding trails,
Through sunlit fields and stormy gales,
I've walked where ancient ruins stand,
And left my prints in foreign sand.

But every place, though strange, feels home,
Each road a story, each step a poem.
For travelers find, in lands afar,
That we all share the same bright star.

A Pantoum: The River's Call

The river calls, a song of old,
Its waters weave through moss and stone.
It carries secrets, soft and bold,
A whispered truth to those alone.

Its waters weave through moss and stone,
A story told in every bend.
A whispered truth to those alone,
A soothing voice, a faithful friend.

A story told in every bend,
It carries secrets, soft and bold.
A soothing voice, a faithful friend —
The river calls, a song of old.

The Ocean's Edge

The horizon blurs,
Sea meeting sky
In an eternal embrace.

Waves crash, retreat,
Whispering secrets
Too ancient to understand.

And I,
A mere speck on the shore, listen.

Blooming Spring

The flowers bloom, the world takes flight,
A tapestry of colors bright.
The birds return with songs anew,
The sky transforms its ashen hue.

The gentle breeze, the soft sunlight,
A season's dance of sheer delight.
The earth revives, its heart beats true,
The flowers bloom.

With every scent, the soul ignites,
Each petal whispers, dreams take flight.
A time of hope, of promise, too,
A vibrant world, reborn for you.
The flowers bloom.

Waves of Time

The shoreline waits for no one,
Each wave carving its story in the sand.
I stood there once,
watching the tide take my footprints away,
As if I had never existed.

But time is not cruel,
It only borrows
What we leave behind—
Memories fading like saltwater mist,
Etching its lessons into our souls.

A Place Called Home

Among the hills where the shadows fall,
There stands a house so quiet, so small.
Its creaking floors, its aging walls,
Still echo with my childhood calls.

The trees outside still whisper my name,
Though years have passed, it feels the same.
A haven of warmth, no need to roam,
For in my heart, it's always home.

One day I'll return when I am free,
To the place where I always long to be.

The Last Goodbye

How do you say goodbye
To someone who still lives in your every thought?
The words catch in your throat,
Like a bird trapped in a cage of unshed tears.

I walked away,
But every step pulled me back.
The echo of your laughter still follows me,
Soft and bittersweet, like a half-forgotten song.
Goodbye, I said, but my heart never learned how.

Laughter at Midnight

Tell me why your laugh
Sounds like the beginning of summer —
The spark before fireworks explode.
And why does your silence feel
Like the calm before a storm?

You're the paradox I can't solve,
The question I don't mind asking again.
And here I am,
At midnight,
Laughing at nothing,
Because it feels like you're still here.

The Path Not Taken

There lies a path through woods untamed,
Where every turn remains unnamed.
Its stones are rough, its thorns unkind,
But treasure waits for those who find.

I stood before its shaded door,
Unsure of what it had in store.
The other road was smooth and bright,
But lacked the thrill of an unknown night.

So, I chose the trail that no one knew,
Its wild embrace and morning dew.
For life's true beauty, I've come to see,
Lies in the risks that set us free.

A Fragment of Us

We were a mosaic,
Pieced together with shards of love and pain.
I thought we were unbreakable,
But even mosaics crack with time.

Now, I hold a fragment of us,
Sharp and glimmering,
Wondering if it's better to bleed from holding on,
Or to let go and lose the light forever.

Midnight Thoughts

The clock strikes twelve,
And the world falls silent,
Leaving me alone with my thoughts.

They spiral like smoke,
Intangible but heavy,
Tracing patterns I can't quite follow.

I wonder if the stars feel this way,
Trapped in the vastness of their own light,
Yearning to break free
But destined to shine.

The Edge of the World

I dreamed of standing at the edge of the world,
Where the sky meets the sea in a quiet embrace.
There, the horizon whispers secrets,
Stories of sailors who chased the unknown.

It calls to me, that endless expanse,
Daring me to leap, to trust, to fly.
For what is life,
If not the courage
To seek the edge of our own fears?

Roots and Wings

You gave me roots when I needed grounding,
When I couldn't see beyond the confines of my world.

And then,
When I grew restless,
When the sky called my name,
You gave me wings.

Now I soar,
But I never forget—
The roots remain,
Always pulling me home.

The Weight of Love

Love is not light—it is heavy,
Like the pull of an anchor beneath the waves.
It grounds us, holds us,
Sometimes drags us down.

But oh, the beauty of its weight—
The way it steadies the heart,
The way it carves us into something new,
Like stone shaped by the patient hand of time.

Love is not perfect—it is flawed,
A tapestry woven with mistakes.
But it is ours,
And that makes it enough.

So let me carry this love with you,
No matter how heavy it becomes.

A Season's Farewell

The leaves fall gently,
Like whispered goodbyes
From the trees that held them
Through countless storms.

Autumn sighs,
Its breath crisp and cool,
A reminder that even endings
Can be beautiful.

The earth prepares for stillness,
But in this pause,
There's a quiet kind of hope,
A promise of renewal.

For even the coldest winter
Will give way to spring.

A Ballad of Shadows

The night was not a void,
But a canvas painted black,
Where whispers roamed like phantoms,
And time never turned back.

The stars were weary candles,
Their flames shivering in the cold.
Each blink spoke of a thousand tales,
All ancient, yet untold.

And in the midst of silence,
I stood with bated breath,
Feeling the weight of forgotten things,
A romance born in death.

But dawn, that cruel betrayer,
Stole the stage with blinding light,
And left me mourning shadows
That danced with me through night.

A Storm's Soliloquy

Do you hear me?
I am the storm tearing across the heavens,
My voice is the howl that shakes your bones,
My tears flood your streets
As I drown the world in fury.

But do you understand me?
I am not anger,
Nor vengeance,
Nor chaos.

I am the cry of a sky long ignored,
A lament for the earth too proud to listen,
A reminder that even the strongest crumble
When the wind whispers their name.

The Forest That Devours

There is a forest where no light dwells,
A place where shadows drink the sun.
The air hums with secrets,
And the ground whispers
of those who dared to run.

The trees stretch like skeletons,
Their branches twisting in disdain.
Each step you take is borrowed time,
Each breath you draw,
A fleeting gain.

The river flows not with water,
But with the tears of those who fell.
Its current drags you forward,
into the heart
Of this verdant hell.

And yet, the beauty beckons,
A trap disguised in emerald hue.
For who could resist the allure
Of what's forbidden
And what's taboo?

But heed this warning, traveler,
before you lose your way.
The forest hungers for your soul—
it's the price you'll have to pay.

The Mirror's Truth

I looked into the mirror today,
And saw a stranger staring back—
Eyes heavy with unspoken truths,
Lips trembling with words unsaid.

"Who are you?" I whispered.
The reflection smirked,
As if amused by my naivety.

"I am the sum of your doubts,"
It replied.
"I am the weight you carry,
The mask you wear,
The silence you fear."

And as I turned away,
It called after me:
"You can't escape yourself,
No matter how far you run."

The Lighthouse
Keeper's Lament

I tend the light atop the cliff,
A solitary, ceaseless task.
The waves below scream their fury,
Their voices hidden behind my mask.

The lantern glows through storms and fog,
A beacon for the lost at sea.
But who will guide the keeper home,
When darkness comes for me?

Each ship that passes never stays,
They vanish into the unknown.
And I remain a lonely watch,
A life carved from stone.

Yet I cannot leave this sacred post,
For who would take my place?
I am bound to this eternal flame,
A shadow lost in space.

So here I stand, both prisoner and guard,
A soul adrift in time.
The lighthouse glows,
But I am dimmed—
A light that's past its prime.

The Fire in the Sky

The comet streaks across the heavens,
A wound in the fabric of the night.
Its light consumes the stars,
A brief rebellion against eternity.

We watch, awestruck,
Wondering if it knows
How fleeting its brilliance is.

But perhaps that is its gift—
To burn brightly,
Without regret,
And vanish before the world
Can dim its fire.

A City of Ghosts

Beneath the moon's indifferent glow,
The city breathes its weary sigh.
Its streets are veins, its towers bones,
A graveyard reaching for the sky.

Once, this place was loud with life,
Its pulse a song, its rhythm fast.
Now it lingers, hollow, quiet—
A relic of a distant past.

The markets hum with ghosts of laughter,
The alleys whisper names long gone.
Each corner holds a fragment of
A story left unfinished, undone.

I walk these streets, a stranger now,
My shadow merging with the night.
The city watches, cold and silent,
Its gaze as sharp as shattered light.

But even ruins have their beauty,
And even ghosts have tales to tell.
This city keeps its secrets close,
A mausoleum of farewell.

A Play of Masks

We wear our masks like armor,
Painted smiles, rehearsed replies.
Each layer hides another wound,
A fragile shield against their eyes.

But underneath, the truth still lingers,
Raw and aching, sharp as glass.
We yearn to shed the roles we play,
To let the world see who we are.

Yet fear keeps us in the shadows,
Our honesty a dangerous thing.
For what if they can't love the face
That hides behind the mask we bring?

Still, there's hope in the quiet moments,
When courage dares to break the chain.
And in the act of baring all,
We find the strength to love again.

A Flame That Won't Burn Out

I am the flame that refuses to die,
The ember buried deep in ash.
You smothered me with silence,
With absence,
With indifference.

But I am not so easily erased.
My fire lives in the cracks of your heart,
In the spaces you thought were empty.

And when the winds rise again,
When your breath fans the coals,
You'll feel my heat—
Not to destroy,
But to remind you:
I am still here.

The Weight of Words

Words are not feathers—they are stones,
Each syllable a weight we bear.
A careless phrase can break the bone,
A whispered truth can strip us bare.

We throw them like pebbles across the sea,
Not knowing where their ripples spread.
But some return, sharp and jagged,
To pierce the skin where love once bled.

And yet, within their brutal strength,
There lies the power to create.
For words can mend as much as a wound,
Their mercy stronger than their hate.

So, speak with care, let kindness guide,
For words endure beyond the grave.
They shape the world we leave behind,
A legacy for those who stay.

The Masquerade

The music swells, and the masks come alive.
Each face, a lie wrapped in glitter,
Each smile, a fortress guarding secrets.

I dance among them,
A shadow moving through the light.
I wonder—do they see me?
Or do they only see the mask I wear?

We are all strangers here,
Lost in a carnival of pretense.
But somewhere beneath the laughter,
A silent yearning calls out—
To be seen, to be known, to be real.

A House of Empty Frames

This house is a gallery of ghosts,
Its walls adorned with empty frames.
Each one a memory you took with you,
Each one a story lost to flames.

The windows stare with hollow eyes,
Their curtains drawn like funeral shrouds.
The echoes of your laughter linger,
A haunting hymn beneath the clouds.

I wander through these barren halls,
A curator of what's been erased.
Your absence hangs like heavy air,
A void no time can ever replace.

But still, I keep the frames intact,
Their emptiness a bitter shrine.
For even though the pictures fade,
They hold the space where you were mine.

The Alchemy of Grief

Grief is an alchemist,
Turning love into lead.
It bends time, stretches seconds
Into eternities of ache.

But even in its cruelty,
Grief is a teacher.
It shows you the fragility of joy,
The weight of moments
You once let slip unnoticed.

And when it has burned you down
To ash and silence,
You find the gold it leaves behind—
A love that endures,
Even in the absence of its source.

The Forgotten Song

Do you remember the song we sang,
The one that carried us through the dark?
Its melody stitched our lives together,
Each note a promise, each chord a spark.

But time has a way of stealing tunes,
Of muting voices, erasing lines.
And now that song lies lost, abandoned,
A memory drowned in a fleeting time.

Yet sometimes, in the quiet hours,
I hear its echo, faint but clear.
And I wonder if you hear it too—
A bridge to bring us back from here.